NIL -Stacks

D0205849

Landmarks of world literature

Emile Zola

L'ASSOMMOIR

UNIVERSITY
OF NEW BRUNSWICK

NOV 29 1996

LIBRARIES

Landmarks of world literature

General Editor: J. P. Stern

EMILE ZOLA

L'Assommoir

DAVID BAGULEY

Professor of French,
The University of Western Ontario

CAMBRIDGE
UNIVERSITY PRESS

Published by the Press Syndicate of the University of Cambridge
The Pitt Building, Trumpington Street, Cambridge CB2 1RP
40 West 20th Street, New York NY 10011-4211, USA
10 Stamford Road, Oakleigh, Victoria 3166, Australia

© Cambridge University Press 1992

First published 1992

Printed in Great Britain at the University Press, Cambridge

A catalogue record for this book is available from the British Library

Library of Congress cataloguing in publication data
Baguley, David.
Emile Zola, L'Assommoir / David Baguley.
        p.   cm. – (Landmarks of world literature)
Includes bibliographical references.
ISBM 0 521 338426 5
1. Zola, Emile, 1840–1902. Assommoir.   I. Title.   II. Series.
PQ2496.B3   1992
843'.8 – dc20   91-43761   CIP

ISBN 0 521 38426 5 hardback

Contents

Acknowledgements

I should like to thank the editorial and production staff of Cambridge University Press for their invaluable assistance in the preparation of this book. I am most grateful too for the generous research grant from the Social Sciences and Humanities Research Council of Canada, which provided me with time and resources to write it. Thanks also to Mónica for an eagle eye and a sympathetic ear.

Note on the text and abbreviations

Page references for the actual text of *L'Assommoir* are taken
from the standard edition of the novel by Henri Mitterand
in Vol. II of *Les Rougon-Macquart* (Paris: Gallimard, 1961),
which appears in the Bibliothèque de la Pléiade format; other
references to this five-volume edition of Zola's series of novels
are preceded by the abbreviation *RM* and the volume number.
For other texts by Zola, references are taken from the fifteen-
volume edition of his *Œuvres complètes* (Paris: Cercle du livre
précieux, 1966–9), also established by Henri Mitterand, and
are preceded by the abbreviation *OC* and the volume number.
All translations from the French are my own. Further bibliographical details for short references appearing in the text are
to be found in the 'Guide to further reading' at the end of
the book.

Chronology

1859	Fails the *baccalauréat*. With grim employment prospects, spends two years leading a bohemian existence in wretched and worsening living conditions in the company of his artist friends.	Italian War. Hugo, *La Légende des siècles*.
1860		Beginnings of the 'liberal Empire'.
1861		Expedition to Mexico.
1862	Finds modest employment with the publisher Hachette and rapidly becomes head of the publicity department. Becomes a naturalised French citizen.	Mexican War. Flaubert, *Salammbô*. Hugo, *Les Misérables*.
1863	Begins a career as a journalist for several newspapers.	Salon des Refusés. Manet, *Le Déjeuner sur l'herbe*.
1864	*Contes à Ninon*.	The First International Working Men's Association founded in London. Baudelaire, *Petits poèmes en prose*. Edmond and Jules de Goncourt, *Germinie Lacerteux*.
1865	Meets his future wife Alexandrine Meley. *La Confession de Claude*, his first novel.	Claude Bernard, *Introduction à l'étude de la médecine expérimentale*.
1866	Leaves Hachette to live (with great difficulty) by his pen. Meets Manet. *Mes haines. Mon salon*.	French troops evacuate Mexico.
1867	*Les Mystères de Marseille. Thérèse Raquin. Edouard Manet*.	Constitutional reforms announced. Universal Exhibition in Paris. Marx, first published volume of *Das Kapital*.
1868	*Madeleine Férat*. Formulates a plan for a series of ten novels, which will become the 20-volume series: *Les Rougon-Macquart*.	
1869		Flaubert, *L'Education sentimentale*.
1870	Marries Alexandrine Meley.	Franco-Prussian War. 2 September: defeat at Sedan; 4 September: fall of the Second Empire; 19 September: Siege of Paris.

1871	*La Fortune des Rougon*, first of the *Rougon-Macquart* novels.	18 March to 28 May: Paris Commune. 31 August: Thiers elected President of the Third Republic.
1872	*La Curée*. Charpentier becomes Zola's publisher. Zola frequents Flaubert's Sunday gatherings.	
1873	*Le Ventre de Paris*.	7 January: death of Napoleon III. 24 May: MacMahon becomes President of the Republic after the resignation of Thiers. German troops leave France.
1874	*La Conquête de Plassans*.	First Impressionist exhibition.
1875	*La Faute de l'abbé Mouret*. Prepares *L'Assommoir*.	
1876	*Son Excellence Eugène Rougon*. 13 April to 7 June: serial publication of the first six chapters of *L'Assommoir* in *Le Bien public*. From 9 July, *La République des Lettres* publishes weekly instalments of *L'Assommoir*.	Mallarmé: *L'Après-midi d'un faune*.
1877	7 January: last instalment of *L'Assommoir* in *La République des Lettres*; the novel appears in book form the same month.	October: legislative elections; republican victory. Hugo, *La Légende des siècles*. Flaubert, *Trois contes*. Edmond de Goncourt, *La Fille Elisa*.
1878	Buys country property at Médan. Establishes close ties with Alexis, Céard, Hennique, Huysmans, Maupassant. *Une Page d'amour*.	
1879	18 January: première of the drama *L'Assommoir*, adapted by Busnach and Gastineau (and Zola), at the Théâtre de l'Ambigu.	Grévy elected President of the Republic. Edmond de Goncourt, *Les Frères Zemganno*.
1880	*Nana*, novel about the life of a courtesan, Nana, daughter of Gervaise and Coupeau. *Le Roman expérimental*, containing Zola's main theoretical writings. *Les Soirées de Médan*, collection of short stories by Zola and his 'disciples'.	Death of Flaubert. Amnesty for the Communards. First Ferry ministry.

1881		Céard, *Une belle journée*. Flaubert, *Bouvard et Pécuchet*. Huysmans, *En ménage*. Verlaine, *Sagesse*. Ministry of Gambetta.
1882	*Pot-Bouille*.	Union Générale crash. Fall from power and death of Gambetta.
1883	*Au Bonheur des dames*.	Maupassant, *Une vie*. Death of the comte de Chambord, the legitimist pretender.
1884	*La Joie de vivre*.	Huysmans, *A rebours*. Trade unions legalised.
1885	*Germinal*, novel on a mining community, with Etienne Lantier, one of Gervaise's sons, as the main character.	Maupassant, *Bel-Ami*. George Moore, *A Mummer's Wife*. Death of Victor Hugo. Grévy re-elected President.
1886	*L'Œuvre*, novel about Gervaise's other son by Lantier, Claude, a painter.	Boulanger Minister of War.
1887	*La Terre*, novel of peasant life, with Jean Macquart, Gervaise's brother, as the main character.	Resignation of Grévy; Sadi Carnot elected President.
1888	*Le Rêve*. Start of lasting liaison with Jeanne Rozerot.	Maupassant, *Pierre et Jean*. Boulangist campaign.
1889	Birth of Denise, daughter of Jeanne Rozerot and Zola.	Universal Exhibition in Paris. Eiffel Tower completed. Flight of Boulanger.
1890	*La Bête humaine*, novel about the railways, with Jacques Lantier, a third son of Gervaise and Lantier, invented for the occasion.	
1891	*L'Argent*, novel on the Paris Stock Exchange and its speculators. Birth of Jacques, son of Jeanne Rozerot and Zola.	Encyclical *Rerum Novarum*. J. Huret, *Enquête sur l'évolution littéraire*. Hardy, *Tess of the d'Urbervilles*. Huysmans, *Là-bas*. Death of Rimbaud.
1892	*La Débâcle*, novel about the Franco-Prussian war and the Paris Commune, with Jean Macquart again as the main character.	

1892–3		Anarchist attacks. Panama scandal.
1893	*Le Docteur Pascal*, last of the *Rougon-Macquart* series.	Death of Taine. Stephen Crane, *Maggie: A Girl of the Streets.*
1894		June: assassination of Sadi Carnot. Casimir-Périer President. Arrest and conviction of Alfred Dreyfus. George Moore, *Esther Waters.*
1895		January: Félix Faure elected President.
1896		Jarry, *Ubu-Roi.*
1897		Campaign in favour of Dreyfus. Barrès, *Les Déracinés.* Gide, *Les Nourritures terrestres.*
1898	13 January: publishes 'J'accuse' in *L'Aurore*. Condemned to a year in prison. 18 July: flees to England. *Paris*, last novel of the trilogy *Les Trois Villes* (*Lourdes, Rome, Paris*).	11 January: acquittal of Esterhazy. 31 August: suicide of Major Henry. Fashoda incident. Huysmans, *La Cathédrale.*
1899	Returns to Paris. *Fécondité*, first of the uncompleted series, *Les Quatre Evangiles* (*Fécondité, Travail, Vérité,* [*Justice*]).	Loubet elected President. L'Action française founded. Return of Alfred Dreyfus from Devil's Island to face trial; declaration of guilt with extenuating circumstances, followed by a presidential pardon.
1902	Night of 28–9 September: dies of 'an accident', asphyxiated by fumes from a blocked chimney in his Paris home.	
1908	Zola's remains are transferred to the Panthéon.	

Introduction

To consider Zola's novel about a washerwoman, Gervaise Macquart, who falls on hard times, takes to drink and dies in abject poverty, a landmark of world literature may seem at first to be an extravagant claim, requiring at least some preliminary justification. Though *L'Assommoir* did not by any means receive universal acclaim from contemporary critics when it first appeared nor for many years thereafter, its exceptional merits have come to be recognised in modern times and there are eloquent testimonies to its importance. Writing for predominantly English readers, one critic, Graham King, has hailed it as 'one of the greatest masterpieces of literature, a work which heralded a new era in the craft of fiction' (*Garden of Zola*, p. 124), whilst the eminent Zola scholar, F. W. J. Hemmings, has described it as an 'indisputable masterpiece', approaching 'sheer artistic perfection', proof alone of all of Zola's works 'against the acid of purely formal criticism' (*Emile Zola*, pp. 113–14). The Belgian critic, Jacques Dubois, who has done most to apply such acid tests, considers it to be 'one of the great events of French literature', a work that has earned its place 'amongst the masterpieces of the modern novel' (Introduction to the Garnier-Flammarion edition, 1969, p. 28). One could go on quoting similar statements, but perhaps the most telling recommendations have come, not just from critics, but from other writers, who, whatever their own artistic tendencies, have admired the artistry of the novel and been moved by its vivid, gripping representations. In Angus Wilson's view, for example, by the mere creation of Gervaise Macquart, '*L'Assommoir* should be judged a great novel' (*Diversity and Depth in Fiction*, p. 102).

One of the most remarkable facts about *L'Assommoir* is that Zola achieved these effects with the simplest of plots.

It was, of course, a fundamental tenet of realist and naturalist writers that complicated plots were to be avoided as contrary to a true picture of life. This was especially true at the time of *L'Assommoir* amongst Zola and his naturalist associates. Flaubert, for example, published his famous story 'A Simple Heart' (in his *Trois contes*), the uneventful life of a domestic servant, the same year as *L'Assommoir* (1877), and his chief disciple, Maupassant, would soon follow suit with his first novel, entitled plainly *Une vie*, the simple life of Jeanne Le Perthuis des Vauds, a socially more privileged existence, but no more fulfilling than that of her humble predecessor. In a similar vein Zola planned to call his novel *The Simple Life of Gervaise Macquart* before he hit upon the far more suggestive title that it now bears. Like the adoption of *The Red and the Black* instead of *Julien* by Stendhal, the change is significant. The dictionary gives 'club' or 'bludgeon', as well as 'grogshop' or 'bar', for *l'assommoir*, but as we shall see, Zola's title can mean much more. The novelist thereby substituted a cryptic title redolent with symbolic meaning that invites a pluralistic reading of the novel for a more patent generic indicator of the biographical model to which the text conforms, one which merely suggested a realistic and literal approach to the work and emphasised the uncomplicated outline of its plot. In his preliminary plans for the novel, in the 'sketch' (*ébauche*) of the work, Zola wrote: 'If I take the title: *La Simple Vie de Gervaise Macquart*, the nature of the book will precisely have to be its simplicity; a story of magnificent starkness, of day-to-day reality, just as it is, without any complications, with very few scenes and the most ordinary ones at that, absolutely nothing that is novelistic or affected.' The novel would be, he added, 'facts strung together, but giving me the *complete life of the people*'.

The novel of Gervaise Macquart's misfortunes is divided appropriately into thirteen chapters. (1) It opens with Gervaise waiting early in the morning in their miserable hotel room, situated in the Goutte-d'Or district of Paris, for her wayward lover, Lantier, who eventually returns, quarrels with the anxious woman and then, whilst she is away doing the laundry in the public washhouse (and fighting with Virginie, the sister of his new mistress, in a famous scene) abandons her with their two children, Claude and Etienne. (2) With typical courage and hard work, at this stage in her life, the laundress recovers from this setback and is nicely making ends meet when she yields to the blandishments of Coupeau, a (temporarily) upstanding roofer from the neighbourhood, whom she agrees to marry despite certain misgivings. (3) The wedding takes place, with lively scenes of popular celebration; (4) Nana is born and the household prospers for some four years until Coupeau, one day, falls off a roof and, (5) losing his taste for work, acquires a taste for strong drink. (6) Gervaise, nevertheless, with the help of a loan from an admirer, the metalworker Goujet, has opened her own laundry, and, despite her husband's lapses, is making it into a going concern, winning the respect of the neighbourhood and Goujet's chaste love. (7) But, in the middle of her birthday feast, rumours of Lantier's return prove to be true; he is invited in to join the party by none other than Coupeau, in the general permissiveness of the celebrations, and, in the following chapter (8), wheedles his way not only into the household, but, if not into her affections, back into Gervaise's favours, for she is repelled by her drunken husband and incapable of repulsing her former lover's advances. (9) Dragged down into destitution by her idle, spendthrift husband and lover, and having lost the respect of Goujet, Gervaise is now forced to yield her shop to her arch-enemy, Virginie, and the latter's husband, Poisson, whilst the conniving Lantier stays on at the shop. (10) In despair at the calamity of her existence, Gervaise herself, despite her earlier resolution, turns to drink and (11) her daughter, Nana, embarks upon an illustrious career as a courtesan. (12) On the verge of starvation, Gervaise wanders the streets begging and vainly trying, in total desperation, to sell her pathetic body. (13) Finally, Coupeau, driven mad by drink, dies in a padded cell in the throes of *delirium tremens*, leaving Gervaise to perish, like a dog, of starvation, filth and exhaustion in a hovel under the stairs of the dilapidated building they occupy.

Such a bald outline of the plot may have a certain usefulness as a guide to new readers of *L'Assommoir*, but it also has certain disadvantages. It does not, to begin with, do justice at all to the powerful realist impact of the novel, to its extraordinary evocative potency. Criticism of late has tended to disregard, even to disparage, the representational aims of realist literature, dwelling upon the arbitrariness of its signs and the artifice of its strategies, questioning its referentiality and its implicit ideology, in short preferring the play of *semiosis* to the constraints of *mimesis*. But the fact remains, and must be emphasised before we embark upon the analytical exercise of criticism and upon the dispersive procedures involved in exploring the different levels, discourses, meanings, of the text, that *L'Assommoir* is a masterly mimetic achievement which grips its readers and holds them in its sway by the intensity of its evocative effects, by its descriptive skills, by the pathos of its characters' plight, by its vivid representation of human foibles and of the brief joys and terrible suffering of its characters, by the sense of doom that hangs over their lives, and by the spells of hope and the defiant intemperance of language and action of these people as they seek to escape the cruel grip of circumstances – indeed by all that contributes in the novel to move all but the most insensate. The French writer Edmonde Charles-Roux has written of the vertiginous, hallucinatory effect that *L'Assommoir* exercises over the reader (*Les Cahiers naturalistes*, 52 (1978), p.9). The novel itself, in a sense, becomes like an *assommoir*, overwhelming the reader with its stunning effects.

A mere outline of the plot also seems to confirm the narrow view of a certain (classical, conservative, elitist, aesthetist) tradition that rejects Zola's novel, along with other naturalist works, as but a gross form of realism, dwelling upon the repulsive aspects of life and written for scandalous effect. In point of fact, no one was more surprised than Zola himself at the *succès de scandale* of his novel, which rapidly brought him fame and fortune after many years of rather indifferent recognition. Yet, whilst Zola no longer had to suffer the killing indifference that he feared, he was immediately faced with a different dilemma, for, as Borges remarked, 'fame is a form of incomprehension, perhaps the worst'.

One final danger consists of failing to recognise that the apparent clarity of design of *L'Assommoir* is thoroughly deceptive. One can emphasise too much the 'classic simplicity' of the work and suggest, like Martin Turnell, that *L'Assommoir* approaches 'the economy and the linear simplicity of the French novels of the classic period' (*The Art of French Fiction*, p. 147), as if the distastefulness and dreariness of much of the novel's content are redeemed by its formal qualities. But, like a landmark, *L'Assommoir* points in several directions and should be viewed from a number of vantage points. Like a landmark too, it both demarcates and is itself set within several boundaries. Since, almost twenty years ago, Jacques Dubois argued that the 'plurality' of Zola's text requires a plurality of approaches (*'L'Assommoir' de Zola*, p. 8), it has been opened up to a variety of perspectives, of which this introductory study will seek to take account and which, in some cases, it will seek to develop. As we explore in turn the social and political significance of the novel, its status as a 'naturalist' work, its particular themes and techniques, and the fascinating story of its reception, we shall attempt to answer, in relation to Zola's novel, the fundamental questions of criticism: what type of text can it be said to be and what can it be said to mean? The answers will inevitably be provisional, but we shall inevitably see also that, with its complexities and its ambiguities, *L'Assommoir* is much more than the picture of a simple life.

Chapter 1

The social and political novel

The setting

Though *L'Assommoir* may be read, enjoyed and studied perfectly well as an independent work, it must also be considered, as Zola insisted in his preface, as part of the twenty-volume series of novels, *Les Rougon-Macquart* (1871–93), the creation of which occupied the better part of his life as a writer. As the series subtitle suggests, *The Natural and Social History of a Family under the Second Empire*, it has a double design: on the one hand, the depiction of contemporary society in its various aspects, a kind of Second Empire *Human Comedy*; on the other hand, a representation (or exemplification) of the workings of the laws of heredity in the lives of members of a single family as they move in that society. In his preliminary notes for the series, Zola tended to emphasise the latter aim. In a page or two of jottings entitled significantly 'Differences between Balzac and myself', for example, he writes: 'My work will be less social than scientific.' But, as the series unfolded during the early years of the Third Republic, the social and historical aims tended to predominate. One essential difference between Balzac's and Zola's series is that, unlike the former's immense fresco of life in the society of the Restoration and the July Monarchy, *The Rougon-Macquart*, notably in *L'Assommoir* and *Germinal*, portray working-class life. In his preliminary notes for the series, Zola, the future novelist-ethnographer, had divided society into four sectors: what he called the 'worlds' of the people (the worker and the soldier), of business (the speculator and the industrialist), of the bourgeoisie ('sons of the parvenus') and high society, along with a disparate class, a 'separate world', to which he consigned the prostitute, the murderer, the priest and the artist. Earlier novelists would have unhesitatingly placed the workers in this last category.

Like the action of a number of *Rougon-Macquart* novels, the events of *L'Assommoir* are roughly contemporaneous with the history of the Second Empire, and the plight of its characters is an implicit indictment of the extravagances of the imperial regime that are depicted directly in other works of the series such as *La Curée* and *Nana*. However, as is the case in most other naturalist novels of the period, there are very few precise indications of the dates of the events of the plot in the text itself, let alone any commentary on the social or historical significance of the action. We can deduce from the allusion by Coupeau to the recent election of Eugène Sue to parliament (28 April 1850) that the opening scene of the novel takes place in May. By following the sometimes vague chronological indications (and with the help of Zola's plans, which are much more informative than the final text), we can establish that Gervaise's wedding takes place at the end of July 1850, that her four years of toil in chapter 4 take us to 1854 and that her birthday feast in chapter 7 occurs on 19 June 1858. By the beginning of chapter 10, she looks back, in 1863, over the thirteen years that have led to her misfortune as she moves into the hovel on staircase B of the tenement-house. In her agony of hunger and desperation at the opening of chapter 12, where she herself begins to lose all sense of time ('It must have been the Saturday after the rent was due, something like the 12th or 13th of January', p. 749), we are, no doubt, in 1869, the year in which she later dies, the year before the fall of the Second Empire. Clearly, in this novel, existential time, time as biological process and a thematised time of fatality and disintegration are far more important than historical events. But the context of Louis Napoleon's regime is by no means irrelevant to the study of *L'Assommoir*, particularly as it affected the conditions of working-class life.

The Second Empire (1852–70) and the curiously elusive figure of Napoleon III have frequently been represented as an almost bizarre parody of the glories of the first Empire. Victor Hugo in exile mercilessly pilloried 'Napoléon le Petit' and it was with reference to the Second Empire that Marx, echoing Hegel, remarked (in the opening sentence of *The Eighteenth*

Brumaire of Louis Bonaparte) that the significant facts of history occur twice, 'the first time as tragedy, the second as farce'. Louis Napoleon's was in many ways an inglorious reign, one of opportunism, repressive political institutions, authoritarianism, police state methods, corruption, hollow pageantry and, in the 1860s, disastrous foreign adventures, a regime designed both to stifle opposition and to cull public favour, thoroughly deserving of the calumnies that writers such as Zola heaped upon it. But, in many respects also, it was a 'progressive' regime, a time of frenzied speculation, investment and economic expansion, which favoured free trade, industrial production, the establishment of large corporations, new banks and a booming stock exchange, the construction of miles of railways and a vast programme of public works, with many of the trappings of a modern capitalist state. Whilst Marx was advocating the dictatorship of the proletariat, Louis Napoleon was claiming to embody the sovereignty of the people. He is said to have held certain socialist views and to have had considerable sympathy for the lot of the workers. In his earlier years he even wrote a pamphlet on the extinction of pauperism. But, as *L'Assommoir* attests, little was done in that direction when he came to power.

The vast programme of public works in the capital that Louis Napoleon instituted under the direction of his protégé, the energetic Alsatian Georges Eugène Haussmann, made 'préfet de la Seine' for the purpose and baron for his troubles, was typical of the régime. The demolition and reconstruction of large areas of Paris were undertaken on the grand scale and precipitated a frenzy of real estate speculation. This reconstruction was good publicity for the régime, recalling earlier transformations during the First Empire. It provided employment for Parisian workers like Coupeau, and for a swelling tide of workers drawn to the city from the provinces like Goujet. But, as contemporary commentators were quick to point out, these public works were not solely in the public interest. The miles of new streets, the long straight avenues, the wide boulevards, had a decidedly strategic practicality for moving troops and repressing insurrection. Furthermore, when the dust had settled on the vast building site that Paris had become, it became clear that, behind the tree-lined avenues and the elegant façades, the sumptuous shops and spacious squares, the long stretches of imposing residences built in the flashy and uniform style so characteristic of the age, there remained, particularly in the outer districts of the city, crowded slums where the deplorable living conditions were made worse by the influx of a whole population displaced from the demolished and renovated districts of the city. Whilst Haussmann could boast of the splendid vistas of the new Paris and his sewage system, his Cloaca Maxima, became a tourist attraction, vast numbers of working-class people, who had contributed their labour to the realisation of his grandiose schemes, were condemned to live in stinking, airless slums.

All this upheaval provides the background to Zola's novel, which is set in the very heart of one such Paris slum. In the opening scene Gervaise watches a vast 'herd' of workers, masons, locksmiths, painters, men of all trades, descending with their tools from the outlying northern districts of the city for their day's work in Paris, an anonymous mass of compliant workers swallowed up menacingly by the city: 'and the crowd surged down into Paris where it was engulfed, continually' (p. 377). In an equivalent scene later in the novel, as she witnesses the return of the troops of exhausted workers near the junction of the boulevard de Magenta and what is now the boulevard Barbès, Gervaise takes stock of the changes that have taken place in her adopted neighbourhood with a significant sense of shame. She sees the dilapidated hovels behind the brand-new houses, the dingy alleys between the sculptured façades: 'Beneath the mounting luxury of Paris was the seething misery of the suburban slums, defiling this huge construction site of a new city, so hastily erected' (p. 764).

The particular slum in which almost all the action of *L'Assommoir* unfolds is the district (or, more appropriately, the neighbourhood, since it covers such a small area) that occupies, on the map, an egg-shaped zone between the Sacré-Cœur and the Gare du Nord, bounded by the rue Polonceau, the boulevard de la Chapelle and the boulevard Barbès (then the rue des Poissonniers), with the rue de la Goutte d'Or running right through the middle. After achieving a certain grim respectability earlier this century (if the photographs give the true picture), the Goutte d'Or has now become once again a bustling neighbourhood of the underprivileged. But the caftan has replaced the cloth cap and the bazaar the 'boozer', as North African immigrants have taken over the streets abandoned by Zola's working-class population. The probable model for the Hôtel Boncœur is now next door to 'Le Maghreb' and the site of old Colombe's establishment is a somewhat less exotic place, a Tati department store. Yet the dilapidated tenements of Zola's day are still largely intact, though they may well finally be coming down in the next phase of modernisation planned for the area.

Apart from its appropriateness as a typical working-class neighbourhood, the Goutte d'Or had certain distinct advantages as a setting for Zola's novel. To begin with, its name (the 'Drop of Gold') had appealing ironic connotations, evoking a rural past when the area was a vineyard and produced prize-winning, health-giving wines, fit for the kings of medieval France, in contrast with the poison concocted in old Colombe's still. The name is also in harmony with the metaphoric and ironic language of the novel, with the elemental imagery of substances and liquids that, as we shall later see, forms much of the thematic texture of the work. The district was also suitably transitional, both subject to change, yet confining its inhabitants, part of the new Paris but also of the undifferentiated *banlieue*, affected by Haussmann's demolitions and a thoroughfare for his mobile armies of workers. The railway, a sign of progress, of escape, or perhaps of further industrial oppressions, ran close by and there were, to the north, both satanic industrial landscapes and the edenic countryside beyond, of which the mean stretch of wasteground, with its withered grass and dead tree (p. 614), the site of the brief courting scene between Gervaise and Goujet ('Gueule d'Or', the 'Man from the North'), gives but a tantalising hint. A prison without walls, the Goutte d'Or was the perfect site to illustrate the conditions of Zola's characters' oppression.

One final advantage of the setting was its convenient proximity to the rue Saint-Georges, where Zola and his wife lived. In the autumn of 1875 the novelist made several expeditions to the area, notebook in hand, to seek information in the usual naturalist manner, compiling a file of observations from his on-site visits and readings that has recently been edited by Henri Mitterand along with Zola's other 'carnets d'enquêtes'. These notes, on the streets, the boulevards, the people, the restaurants, the trades of the area, offer a fascinating series of varied impressions in which the authentic details of what Zola observed (and read) are economically recorded and filtered according to the needs of the future novel. Thus the blue flowers on the wallpaper of a real laundry will take on a symbolic purpose in the novel as a sign of Gervaise's hope; the stinking abattoirs which, in 1875, were no longer in existence, are linked in these notes to the Lariboisière hospital, which was being built under the Second Empire and on which Coupeau, in fact, spends his working days, to form the significant boundaries of Gervaise's entrapment and fate. In the novel, the 'grande maison' will seem immensely larger and more menacing to Gervaise than the one that Zola describes in these notes. Once again, as with the historical background, the novel will draw discreetly upon authentic details to produce significant and signifying effects. Rather than recreating a locale, Zola was more intent upon creating a milieu suitable for illustrating the main social aims of his work, as he clearly expressed them in the opening passage of his *ébauche*:

Show the milieu of the people and explain by this milieu the way of life of the people: how it is that, in Paris, drunkenness, the dissolution of families, fighting, the acceptance of all kinds of shame and misery, arise from the very living conditions of the workers, from the hard grind, the overcrowding, the neglect, etc. ... A terrible picture which will convey its own message.

The workers' condition

This was not by any means Zola's first contact with working-class life, nor the first time that he had written about it. He had himself suffered the miseries and indignities of unemployment, extreme want, even near-starvation, during his lean early years in Paris. He had working-class relatives on his mother's side of the family, like his uncle Adolphe Aubert, a house-painter, whose daughter, Anna, had given her parents similar concerns to those that Nana causes the Coupeaus in the novel. As a journalist under the Second Empire, Zola had written movingly about the plight of the workers, calling for better conditions, more air and space, to counteract the fatal attractions of the bars (in *La Tribune* of 18 October 1868, for example), or, in his articles for *Le Rappel* and *La Cloche*, vehemently attacking the corruption of the imperial regime by contrasting the extravagances of the rich with the sufferings of the poor (*OC* XIII, 258–9, 266). He had been no less unbridled in his attacks on the conservative government of the early years of the Republic. In *La Cloche* of 28 March 1872, for example, in opposing the so-called *loi Roussel* introduced to clamp down on drinking, he assailed the legislators for serving the interests of the distillers at the expense of the people; in *Le Corsaire* of 17 December 1872, he defended the right of overtaxed, dehumanised workers to drink wine, denouncing the drunken pleasures of the ruling classes, arguing pointedly against the prevailing bourgeois view that the revolutionary spirit of the age 'stems from a badly corked litre bottle and that the great legal conquests of '89 were gathered up in the slops of the cheap bar' (*OC* XIV, 199). It was to the government itself that he attributed the blame for the alcoholic excesses of the worker:

If he slips, if he rolls into drunkenness, it is your fault. Do you not want him to be stupid, drunk with ignorance, like an animal? So he enters a bar, turns to the only joy that he has at hand, takes it to excess, because you close up his horizons and because he needs a dream, even if it is the dream of intoxication.   (*OC* XIV, 200)

Zola's final article for *Le Corsaire* ('Le lendemain d'une crise', 22 December 1872), was a savage, courageous indictment of the government, drawing again upon an effective strategy, setting the sufferings of the starving family of an unemployed worker against the political ambitions and extravagant indulgences of the powerful. The newspaper was suspended and Zola's voice was silenced, at least for the time being, in the Parisian press. The political message of *L'Assommoir* is much more ambiguous than it was in these polemical articles, but there is no doubting Zola's credentials as a committed political writer and as a defender of the rights of the underprivileged.

In preparing his novel about what he would later call in his preface 'the foul environment of our suburbs' and about their unfortunate inhabitants, Zola did not rely entirely upon his own experience and observations. He took notes, for example, on a curious volume of sociological analysis entitled *Question sociale. Le Sublime, ou le travailleur comme il est en 1870 et ce qu'il peut être* (1870), written by a former worker, Denis Poulot, who had done well enough for himself to become a boss. In the second part of his book, on 'what the worker can be', Poulot advocates, not surprisingly, with earnest reformist zeal, a collaborative effort by the labouring classes and their bosses for the improvement of the workers' lot. As well as borrowing from this work several picturesque details, the idea for certain scenes (like the visit to the Louvre in chapter 3) and certain choice expressions of Parisian slang, Zola was particularly interested in the first part of the book (on 'the worker as he is in 1870') where Poulot presents a curious typology of Parisian workers at the time. Using ironically an expression from the chorus of an edifying song by Tisserand ('God, that sublime worker') to name certain of his categories, Poulot divides his working men into eight different types: (1) 'the true worker'; (2) 'the worker'; (3) 'the mixed worker'; (4) 'the simple sublime'; (5) 'the faded and fallen sublime'; (6) 'the true sublime'; (7) 'the son of God'; (8) 'the sublime of sublimes'. The system works in descending order of merit, ranging from the conscientious, skilled, 'true worker', the model citizen, bent on self-betterment, with his republican interest in politics for the peaceful improvement of society, down to the 'sublime' categories of idle alcoholics or of political agitators, sober but dangerous elements.

Though there is disagreement amongst critics about the extent to which Zola applied Poulot's typology in *L'Assommoir*, there is definitely a similar gallery of types in Zola's novel. Goujet is clearly the paragon, industrious, abstemious, neat and tidy in body and mind, a moderate republican, 'wisely so, in the name of justice and of the happiness of all' (p. 475), though he lacks the educational interests of Poulot's first type, preferring to cut out pictures rather than read books (pp. 473–4). Coupeau starts near the top of the scheme, but, after his fall, when his resolutions fade, he slides dramatically down the scale to join the ranks of his 'sublime' drinking mates, like Mes-Bottes, Bibi-la-Grillade and Bec-Salé, whose names, incidentally, came straight from Poulot's study. As for Lantier, a figure almost too bad to be true, he would, no doubt, qualify as a 'son of God', a self-styled champion of the proletariat, with a little learning to his name and no little authority over others, a man infinitely more generous with his words than with his deeds, whose platform Zola sets forth in a distinctly ironical, Flaubertian manner, as he describes Lantier one day angrily thumping his pile of newspapers and roaring: 'I want the suppression of militarism, the brotherhood of nations ... I want the abolition of privileges, titles and monopolies ... I want equal wages, a fair distribution of profits, the glorification of the proletariat ... All the freedoms, do you hear me! All! ... And divorce!' (p. 606). As Pierre Cogny and Geoff Woollen have pointed out, Zola applied the system more freely and more discreetly than has usually been supposed, mixing the categories to some degree, refraining from using Poulot's terminology and making imaginative use of his source. But there were enough traces of *Le Sublime* in *L'Assommoir* for one Paris newspaper, *Le Télégraphe*, to splash across its front page (on 17 March 1877) an accusation of plagiarism, backed up by a whole series of (largely spurious) comparisons between the two works. In a letter to the director of the newspaper, Auguste Dumont, which appeared the next day, Zola replied, *con altura*, that the charge was comical, openly indicating his other sources and explaining that he always borrowed from documentary works for his novels, just as he borrowed from life. 'What is well and truly mine', he concluded, 'are my characters, my scenes, the life of my work, and that is the whole of *L'Assommoir*.'

Politics in the novel

Just as significant perhaps as the detailed borrowings from Poulot's text and the view of the Paris worker that the novelist derived from what he considered to be an authoritative study is the very fact that Zola should see the need to draw upon such sources. As well as notes from *Le Sublime*, there is in the preparatory dossier of the novel a newspaper cutting of an article by Francisque Sarcey (from *Le Gaulois* of 18 February 1870) written in a similar vein, claiming to define three different types of workers: the idle, complaining, political agitator; the ideal workman, who is sober, assiduous, reliable; and the more typical worker, a carefree, wasteful and improvident individual, whom Sarcey urges to mend his ways to improve his condition. The paternalistic attitudes that inform these texts and their elementary sociological posture clearly reveal the considerable distance or alienation between the writer and the people that he seeks to depict, which is not only a fundamental feature of *L'Assommoir* according to certain critics, but is also a recurrent problem in the interpretation of proletarian literature, as debates on populist literature and social realism in the twentieth century have shown. Can the (inevitably?) 'bourgeois' writer adequately represent (in both senses of the term) the working classes? Must the writer be of the people and for the people to write about the people? Is it possible to describe objectively, realistically, sociologically, the miseries and manners of the poor without some degree of complicity in the perpetuation of their condition? Should proletarian literature, David Caute asks (*The Illusion*, p.56), 'be defined and consecrated in terms of (a) the class origins of the writer, (b) the *milieu* described in the play or novel, or (c) the ideological perspective of the work'? There have been long-standing differences of opinion amongst readers and critics of *L'Assommoir* on the interpretation of the novel's social and political message, more precisely on two crucial questions: on the degree to which the novel presents a

true picture of working-class life and on the political implications and (likely) impact of the work. The very terms and order
in which conflicting views on these issues are presented con-
stitute in themselves, of course, a commitment by the critic
on these issues. But the model of legal procedure allows one,
conveniently, to begin with the charges.

Even before the novel had appeared in full, Zola found
himself embroiled in controversy. It was customary in Zola's
day to pre-publish novels in serial form in the press, a practice
that Zola deplored, though not enough to renounce the financial
advantages and the publicity that this form of publication
afforded. Particularly irked by the mangling of his text in this
way, the author of *L'Assommoir* wrote (to Ludovic Halévy
on 24 May 1876) that he wished he could place an announce-
ment in the press before each serialised version appeared:
'My literary friends are asked to wait for the volume before
reading this work.' The first six chapters of *L'Assommoir*
appeared in 42 instalments in a recently radicalised republican
newspaper, *Le Bien public*, whose sales its director, Yves
Guyot, hoped substantially to increase by publishing Zola's
novel. When it seemed to be having the opposite effect and
it was clear that Zola's picture of Parisian manners did not
correspond to the radical politics of the newspaper, publication
was stopped. It took up again a month later in a literary
weekly, *La République des lettres*, allied to *Le Bien public*
and directed by the Parnassian poet Catulle Mendès, but not
without incident. When a public prosecutor intervened to
prevent an instalment of the novel appearing in a special
number of the journal, Mendès promised Zola that, if necessary,
he would be prepared to print future numbers in Belgium.
Left-wing publications were still being closely scrutinised by
the authorities at the time. Yet the left-wing newspapers were
no less condemnatory than their conservative counterparts
when the novel appeared. Whereas, for example, the conservative critic of *La Gazette de France* called the author of
L'Assommoir 'the leader of the literary Commune', the
republican Arthur Ranc, still in exile for his part in the Commune and writing anonymously for *La République française*,

condemned Zola's 'Nero-like scorn for the people' in his review of the novel. In fact, ironically, at least one right-wing newspaper, *Le Figaro*, praised the novel, in an article by Albert Wolff (5 February 1877), for its lack of political dissent and for not 'rendering society responsible for the evils of the slums', whereas the left-wing *La Tribune*, which was sponsoring a workers' congress in October 1876, came out against Zola's proletarian novel in the same month (15 October 1876) for the degrading picture of the workers that it supposedly presented. In a survey of the reception of *L'Assommoir* in the Parisian press, Pierre Boutan has shown the remarkable degree to which literary assessments of the novel were politically motivated. Unlike Hugo's play *Hernani* and the legendary battle earlier in the century, to which the controversy over the publication of *L'Assommoir* has often been compared, Zola's novel succeeded in pleasing neither the progressive nor the reactionary factions. Whatever praise it did receive, at least in the press, was largely prompted by the wrong reasons.

Later commentators have frequently questioned on political grounds the representative nature of Zola's depiction of working-class life and, in particular, the ideological orientation that the novel implies. Zola's proletariat, it has been argued, is almost entirely without a political conscience or a political memory. There had been barricades in the rue de la Goutte d'Or in 1848, and the very bars in which Zola's workers drink themselves into a stupor were frequently the scene, particularly towards the end of the Second Empire, of clandestine political meetings. Zola's Goutte d'Or seems totally impervious to even the news of the strikes that were taking place elsewhere in Paris, the public disturbances and the political propaganda which were widespread under the Empire, the improvements in working-class education and awareness at that time. There is no mention, for example, of the establishment of the French chapter of the First International in Paris in 1865, nor of the political unrest that preceded the fall of the Second Empire in 1870 and the Commune in 1871. There is evidence also, according to the historian Jeanne Gaillard, that in contradiction with the dominant theme of Zola's novel, the deteriorating state of working-class life, the conditions of the urban poor, though never enviable, marginally improved during the Second Empire, with wages rising by some 30 per cent. Zola undoubtedly dwells upon the darker side of working-class life.

This is particularly true of what many critics and translators have taken to be the novel's major theme. Drunkenness, though not to be denied as a serious social problem, becomes in *L'Assommoir* a way of life. A reading of the novel seems to suggest that Zola too readily subscribed to the prevailing bourgeois view, backed up by social reformers and medical experts, that the demon drink was the primary cause of proletarian misery. Were idle boozers like Mes-Bottes and Bec-Salé, Poulot's 'sublimes', really typical 'workers', or do they merely correspond to a stereotyped bourgeois view? In preparing his novel, Zola took down a few pages of notes on a recent study of alcoholism by Dr Valentin Magnan, entitled *De l'alcoolisme, des diverses formes du délire alcoolique et de leur traitement* (1874), for his own study of Coupeau's condition. According to Magnan, however, alcoholism was more of a problem in the provinces, particularly in rural areas, than in Paris. Yet Coupeau is temporarily cured of his condition when he goes to work for three months in Etampes. As the narrator explains: 'People just don't realise how much drunkards are restored by leaving the air of Paris, where there is a haze of wine and spirits in the streets' (p. 673)! In Zola's novel, drink seemingly becomes less a social problem or a symptom of social ills than an environmental hazard. The chief doctor at the Sainte-Anne hospital, where her husband is confined (and where, incidentally, Dr Magnan had studied the phenomenon), interrogates Gervaise with his piercing gaze and his scientific detachment, as she watches in horror Coupeau's convulsions, and pronounces his fatal sentence: 'You drink! You'd better watch out. See what drinking leads to … One of these days you'll die like that' (p. 786). Zola has been blamed for limiting his novel, particularly after Coupeau's accident, to the depiction of the fatal effects of alcoholism instead of painting a broader picture of working-class life.

Zola has also been severely criticised for presenting, not

only an incomplete picture of proletarian life, but even a caricature of proletarian attitudes, particularly again in political matters, precisely at a time when the labouring classes were organising themselves into a coherent political force. Political discussion amongst his workers goes little further than Coupeau's apathetic outburst at the wedding feast: 'Now there's a real farce for you, politics! Is it anything to do with us? ... They can do what they like, have a king, an emperor, nothing at all, for all I care, it won't stop me earning my five francs and eating and sleeping, will it? ... No, it's all stupid!' (p. 455). The most politically active character in the novel, Lantier, is a rogue, with his cliché-ridden demagoguery, his half-baked notions, his vague socialism masking a ruthless spirit, a character as insinuating and self-serving in his politics as he is in his social and sexual behaviour. The advice that he 'declaims' to his son, Etienne, the day the boy leaves to work in Lille, rings doubly hollow for its hypocrisy: 'Remember that the producer is not a slave, but that whoever is not a producer is a parasite' (p. 608). Several shades of opinion are represented by characters in the novel – Lorilleux, the legitimist, Poisson, the Bonapartist policeman, whom Lantier cruelly mocks, calling him 'Badingue' (a distortion of Napoleon III's nickname, Badinguet, with emphasis on *dingue*, meaning 'barmy'), Madinier, a republican who nevertheless admires the Emperor – but they are all presented in a *reductio ad absurdum* of political opinion. Debate in the 'Assommoir' itself, old Colombe's establishment, takes place in a drunken haze and rapidly degenerates into salacious anecdotes (p. 627). Goujet would seem to be the exception, at least in that his political vision is not clouded by drink, but, for all his republican convictions, he remains politically ineffectual. As his timely intervention saves the merely curious Coupeau from trouble behind a barricade in the 2 December insurrection against Louis Napoleon's *coup d'état* (p. 475), he wonders if he should have played a more active part in the proceedings, but, despite his scruples, he involves himself in the events no more than the indifferent, dismissive Coupeau. There is, therefore, barely a hint of political consciousness in Zola's workers, who are far more interested in drinking parties than in political parties, in publicans than republicans.

To Zola's claim that he had based his study on solid documentary evidence, his critics would nowadays tend to retort that, just as there can be no neutral, objective history, there can be no pure sociology, not even in the naturalist novel, despite the impression of an unmediated contact with the raw data of life that the realist text conveys. Realist discourse, as critics like Roland Barthes have famously shown, only appears to be ideologically innocent. Its realistic devices serve to naturalise and to pass off as reality itself an idea of reality with its unstated ideological presuppositions. Zola shared the naive epistemological confidence of his age in believing that historical and social truth could be objectively represented. Hence his claim, in the preface to *L'Assommoir*, that the truth of his novel was in itself a defence against his detractors. 'My work will defend me', he wrote. 'It is a work of truth, the first novel about the people which does not lie and which has the true smell of the people.' He was equally confident about his sources. In reply to the charge of plagiarism, he wrote to the director of *Le Télégraphe* (16 March 1877) that *Le Sublime* was 'a book of documents whose author quotes words that have been heard and true facts. To borrow something from it is to borrow from reality.' But the novelist also borrowed, or, more likely, found confirmation of a set of attitudes towards the working class that were commonplace in Zola's times. Henri Mitterand, with this problem in mind, has interestingly compared *L'Assommoir* with the implicit view of the worker contained in Pierre Larousse's famous *Grand Dictionnaire universel du XIXe siècle* (1874), the dictionary being another supposedly objective, documentary record that is in reality, as Flaubert mockingly showed, another source of received ideas. There is the same stereotyping of workers into 'good' and 'bad', 'lazy' and 'diligent', definitions and quotations which express 'a virtuous and moving humanitarianism, which does not shirk before depicting working-class sufferings, but merely to deplore the moral consequences and to come up with no other remedy than an appeal to the foresight, the generosity and the imagination of the ruling classes' (*Le Regard et le signe*, p. 218). Similarly, Jacques Dubois has compared *L'Assommoir* to the paternalistic discourse of certain bourgeois social reformers of the age, in which emphasis is also placed on the problematic intemperance of the workers ('*L'Assommoir' de Zola*, pp. 116–19). The aristocratic or romantic view of proletarian life as an exotic underworld is replaced in the course of the nineteenth century by a vision of an antithetical bourgeois world of neglect, immoderation and prodigality. Yet, complicating this view in Zola's novel is the (apparently) rigorous logic of the demonstration, the inexorable pattern of events, the 'fatal downfall' (in the novelist's own words), which brings his characters to a state of inevitable degradation. Like the animals in the abattoirs or the victims in the hospital, the very social condition of the workers in Zola's novel would seem to condemn them to a fatal *assommage*.

But the most serious criticism of *L'Assommoir* along these lines has come, as one might expect, from the communist left, judgements that are frequently tempered by a hint of regret, for Zola has been held by certain marxist commentators to be a progressive writer for his courageous part in the Dreyfus affair and, above all, for his other proletarian novel, *Germinal* (1885), which deals directly with the class struggle, industrial action and capitalist exploitation of the workers. For them, *L'Assommoir* is an enormous error of judgement. Such critics, of course, believe in both the capacity and the responsibility of literature to 'reflect' and represent an objective reality, the reality of the class struggle. Thus Henri Barbusse, a founder of the Association of Revolutionary Writers and Artists in 1932, writing about *L'Assommoir* the same year, points to the serious lack in Zola's 'moving story' of any analysis of the causes of the dreadful evil that he depicts. The novel's outlook, according to Barbusse, remains 'hopeless, issueless, purely negative', offering no remedies, 'no weapon of destruction against a wicked order except the indirect destructive virtue possessed by all truthful works' (*Zola*, pp. 109–10). Barbusse has no faith in the goodwill of the moralists and legislators to whom Zola's novel is an indirect appeal, a novel which he unfavourably compares with a work that, in his view, played a real social role, *Uncle Tom's Cabin*. For the communist critic, Jean Fréville, an associate of Barbusse, *L'Assommoir* is exceptionable because it attributes the blame for the workers' abominable conditions to the workers themselves, to their idleness and lax moral standards. The solution that the novel proposes is for the worker to enter the bourgeoisie, open a little shop like Gervaise. Zola's 'ideal' in *L'Assommoir* is reactionary, pandering to the bourgeois view of the proletariat as a drunken, good-for-nothing rabble, who beat their wives and children and are led astray by tap-room orators, an ignorant, incompetent populace that should be kept in its place. Fortunately, in Fréville's view (in *Zola, semeur d'orages*, pp. 100−5), Zola learnt his lesson, and wrote *Germinal*. Writing more recently, and even less compromisingly, in the left-wing French journal, *Europe* (nos. 83−4 (November−December 1952)) − to take one final example − André Kédros addressed an open letter to the author of *L'Assommoir* (on the 50th anniversary of his death!), asserting that Zola's novel confirms and legitimises bourgeois scorn for the people: 'And your protestations of innocence, and the good intentions that you invoked a posteriori are of no avail: despite *Germinal*, despite your subsequent political evolution, *L'Assommoir* has remained one of the most enormous *misunderstandings* of literary history' (p. 66).

The living author himself was always most reluctant to draw political inferences from *L'Assommoir*, particularly at the time of the publication of the novel, when he was publicly advocating the objective, scientific, documentary value of naturalist literature. 'I do not intend to be a socialist,' he had written in the 1869 plan for his series of novels, 'but simply an observer and an artist' (*RM* V, 1757). But, when pressed by adverse criticism, particularly from republican critics, he felt compelled to reply in a long letter to the director of *Le Bien public*, Yves Guyot, dated 10 February 1877. Expressing scorn for idealist politicians and denying that the workers in his novel are merely idle drunkards, he wrote:

If one wanted absolutely to force me to draw conclusions, I would say that the whole of *L'Assommoir* can be summed up in this one sentence: close the taverns, open up the schools. Drunkenness is destroying the people. Look at the statistics, go into the hospitals, conduct an inquiry, you will see if I am lying. Whoever could put an end to drunkenness would do more for France than Charlemagne and Napoleon. Let me add also: clean up the slums and increase wages. The question of living conditions is vital; the stench from the street, the sordid staircase, the tiny room in which fathers and daughters, brothers and sisters, sleep all together, are the major cause of depravity in the slums. Back-breaking work that reduces man to the level of the beast, insufficient wages that discourage him and make him look for ways to forget his plight, these are what fill the taverns and the brothels. Yes, the people are this way, but because that is the way society wants them to be.

At this stage (and for most of his life), Zola was a moderate reformer, a progressive republican, with as much suspicion of revolutionaries as scorn for the politicians in power. On the workers' congress of 1876, he had written in *Le Sémaphore de Marseille* (10 October 1876): 'My opinion is that this anger of one class against another can serve no fruitful purpose. Since the workers have got together to make known the evils from which they suffer and to seek remedies for these evils, they should remain within the practical part of their programme, without provoking civil war.' The memory of the Commune was still very fresh.

In fact, this may be one of the major reasons why Zola not only refrained from writing a novel of political advocacy, but even censored its political content himself. In the very first stages of the conception of *L'Assommoir*, he intended, according to an early note, to deal with 'politics and the people, with their chatter, their tales of forty-eight, their misery and hate of the rich, their sufferings' (see *RM* II, 1541). He later dropped any reference to the photograph of a worker killed on the barricades in 1848, which he had earlier intended to include. To a considerable extent, however, by doing so, as we see at the beginning of *L'Assommoir*, Zola was following the interpretations of republican historians of the time, who recorded the relative lack of resistance amongst the Parisian workers against Louis Napoleon's *coup d'état* and, at the outset, against his régime. As Alfred Cobban, following on the tradition, has more recently written: 'The masses were on the side of the dictator' (*A History of Modern France*, Vol. II (Harmondsworth: Penguin, 1961), p. 155). Zola was, after all, writing history, but, at the same time, he was writing after the Commune. He was fully aware, as we saw earlier, that, in the wake of the Commune, the ruling classes equated insurrection and alcoholism. Susanna Barrows writes on this point that 'from the anguish of foreign and civil war emerged the myth, sturdy and none too subtle, of the habitually drunken, politically dangerous commoner' (*Consciousness and Class Experience in Nineteenth-Century Europe*, p. 208); alcoholism was a 'code-word' for working-class rebellion, Jacques Bonhomme (the typical worker) a drunkard, and alcoholic excess an excuse for political repression. By concentrating on his depiction of the misery of working-class conditions, by writing a social rather than a political novel, Zola avoided nurturing the 'myth'.

Though overt political commentary is almost entirely absent from *L'Assommoir*, there are, nevertheless, undoubtedly more political allusions in the novel than might at first be supposed, even where they might be least expected. In the birthday celebration scene of chapter 7, for example, the ceremonial dismemberment of the goose by the Bonapartist policeman, Poisson, an old soldier and the only guest with skill at arms, 'his eyes staring at the beast, as if to nail it to the bottom of the plate' (p. 577), has about it, despite the hilarity of the episode, a sinister allegorical potential, which was not lost on the caricaturist, André Gill, who drew Poisson ('Badingue') with the unmistakable features of Badinguet in the illustrated edition of the novel. The patriotic joke by Lorilleux that follows the operation ('Ah! what if it was a Cossack, eh!') is as inapt as it is inept in the presence of old Bru, who has recently lost three sons in the Crimean War. The ditties that the revellers later sing, at a time when even the songs in the 'cafés-concerts' were censored (and therefore coded), are, as Robert Lethbridge has shown, far more political and revolutionary than they seem. And, as the public prosecutor's intervention with *La République des Lettres* suggests, Zola's so-called reactionary, bourgeois novel was in itself sufficient cause for concern even to the authorities of the Third Republic.

Zola's achievement, then, is to have represented, as never

before, the cruel reality of the abominable conditions of working-class life, in defiance of the theories and conceptions of reactionary or radical politicians alike, or of well-meaning social reformers, who would gloss over the hideous squalor of the slums with edifying invocations and idealised pictures of the common man. For Zola the writer's task was to cut through the rhetoric, reveal the truth in all its horror, expose the sores of society. As he wrote (9 September 1876) to Albert Millaud, another severe critic of his novel: 'I am not a painter of idylls, I consider that the only way to attack evil is with a red-hot iron.' Zola was aware that he had to follow a fine line between the temptation to moralise and the tendency to politicise, between the temperance tract and political propaganda. 'Don't flatter the worker', he reminded himself in his *ébauche*, 'and don't blacken him. An absolutely exact reality.' If Zola carefully avoided the overtly political, he just as carefully tried to avoid the manifestly moral. He warned himself in his notes not to 'lapse into the *Manuel*', in reference to a type of edifying literature exemplified by Eugène Manuel's play, *The Workers* (*Les Ouvriers*, 1870), reviewed by Sarcey in the article mentioned above, a play in which an ideal worker denounces the evils of drink in alexandrines! The only concession to the genre is, perhaps, Goujet, who is apparently the only good apple in the barrel, a figure whose virtuousness bothered Zola himself as much as it has puzzled the novel's critics. Yet, for all his merits, Goujet achieves neither prosperity nor happiness, only an unhappy fate that confounds the moralists' law that goodness is rewarded. Indeed, in a more general way, *L'Assommoir* was written to countervail a whole tradition of stereotyped representations of the labouring classes, a whole gallery of romance figures: the comic rascal, the noble pariah, the paragon and the beast, set in an underworld of intrigue and adventure, the characters of Eugène Sue's *Mysteries of Paris* or of Victor Hugo's *Les Misérables*, the stuff of comic and romantic opera. Significantly, Hugo himself was reported to have expressed strong disapproval of *L'Assommoir* in terms which, ironically, vindicate Zola's purpose: 'You do not have the right to show misery and misfortune in all its nakedness' (see *RM* II, 1563).

A woman's lot

L'Assommoir, therefore, could be described as a powerful, original work of realist representation, based upon a consider-able (but far from total) familiarity with working-class condi-tions, a work of sociological rather than political orientation which nevertheless contains a strong indictment of the prevailing social system, without being free from certain presuppositions about the people — presuppositions that have proved to be objectionable when scrutinised by the more perceptive political commentators on Zola's novel. This profile of *L'Assommoir* could be readily applied to the 'view' of women that the novel presents. Zola thoroughly documented himself in his 'carnet d'enquête' on the working conditions of women in the chosen milieu, on the washhouse, the laundry, the charges for washing and ironing every item of clothing, the wages of the laundry worker, her meagre budget. Gervaise was already a laundress before coming to Paris, as we see in *La Fortune des Rougon* (1871); so it is unlikely that, as has been suggested, the choice of her occupation would have been determined by the more recent pictorial representations of laundresses by impressionist artists, notably Degas, whom Zola knew. The laundry setting does provide more of the most picturesque scenes in the novel, but the choice was even more appropriate for the themes of the work. Though alcoholism in Zola's society was less a problem amongst the working women than amongst the men, the wretched conditions in which laundresses worked frequently drove them to drink. But laundering was also significantly a female occupation with a reputation for moral laxity. Laund-resses were an important part of their community and belonged to an extraordinarily extensive industry. This vast population of female workers was exploited not only for their labour but also for their sexuality. The harsh conditions of the laundress, her pittance of a wage, her enforced recourse to drink and prostitution, are ignored in titillating representations of her sensuality: half-undressed in the steamy heat of her shop, admitted to the intimacy of the bachelor's quarters, sexually accessible, clean and fresh, exposing underwear and flesh, objects of fantasy and fetishism. There is undeniably more than a hint of prurience in Zola's presentation of the women workers in his novel, not only the young laundresses like the dissolute Clémence in Gervaise's shop, but also the artificial flower-makers like Nana and her friends. There is a lascivious male gaze, actualised in certain scenes: the wide-eyed boy, Charles, watching Gervaise spank Virginie's bare buttocks in the famous washhouse battle scene (p. 400); Coupeau languidly enjoying the sight of the sweating women at work, baring their flesh; the anonymous male passer-by peeking into the shop at night and taking away a 'momentary vision of bare-breasted female workers bathed in a reddish mist' (p. 517).

But, at the same time, *L'Assommoir* offers a moving testimony to the plight of the female worker, to her exploitation and her enforced submissiveness, her long hours of toil, her suffering in brutal scenes of domestic violence, the crushing burden that she bears in coping with the impossible task of keeping a household together, providing for the children who depend upon her and for the men who abuse her. The story of Gervaise's troubles seems almost contrived to illustrate the problem of the dependency of the working-class woman on the men with whom she associates. A victim of her early circumstances in Lantier's company and of her later misfortune with Coupeau, Gervaise is ruined by a combination of her natural submissiveness and her social subservience to the men in her life. The ironic turns that her relationships take graphically demonstrate the uncertainties and pitfalls of the female worker's condition. When Lantier has left her penniless and with two children to keep at the beginning of the novel, she fares much better without him. Yet he returns to finish her off. Coupeau seems to be a good prospect at first, particularly once he has assured her of his sober habits. Yet he turns out to be the opposite of her expectations and to confirm her worst fears. Ironically, also, her moral scruples prevent her from eloping with Goujet and from escaping from her infernal domestic situation: two children and a mother-in-law to support as well as the two men who beat her. In chapter 9, almost at the end of her tether, she bemoans her fate: 'two men on her back, to look after and satisfy, it was often more than she could stand. Good God! one husband is already enough to wear you out!... On the days when they came home in a foul temper, they would take it out on her. Here we go! give her a good thrashing' (p. 647). Gervaise can only submit. 'By the end of the week her head was spinning and she ached all over; she was in a daze and wild-eyed. That kind of life just wears a woman out' (p. 648). With familiar resignation she reasons that things could be worse: 'And she found her situation natural; there were so many in the same boat; she tried to find a little bit of happiness all the same' (p. 648). The typicality of Gervaise's situation is underlined in other scenes: when the cries of battered wives are heard along the corridors of the tenement building; when she joins the ranks of desperate women waiting to intercept the men as they leave the roofing works (on the rare occasions when Coupeau is amongst them), 'other poor creatures, wives on the watch to prevent the wages from flying off to the tavern' (p. 761); even when she joins the ranks of the prostitutes, the 'women on guard in the night, as if they were planted from one end to the other of the outer boulevards' (p. 771). In view of the experiences of Zola's heroine, it is hardly surprising that, in his theatrical adaptation of *L'Assommoir* (called *Drink*), Charles Reade should invent a female character, Phoebe Sage, who acts as a foil to Gervaise and declares at the start of the play: 'I've the good luck not to be encumbered with the assistance of a man' (Act I, scene 1).

However, despite the disadvantages and notwithstanding Nana's nascent female bestiality, Virginie's natural treachery or the vindictiveness of the gossips of the Goutte d'Or, it is the female characters of the novel alone, Gervaise, Lalie Bijard, even Madame Goujet, who find the strength and courage to struggle against the appalling conditions that oppress them. Zola was no Flora Tristan, a defender of working women's rights, any more than he was a Robert Tressell (author of *The Ragged Trousered Philanthropists*), but he presents in *L'Assommoir* a poignant picture of the working woman's condition.

Ambiguities

If, as Sandy Petrey has recently argued, 'the progressive implications of Zola's introduction of workers into the novel are
countered by the reactionary effect of a narrative representing
workers as dissolute and irresponsible' (*A New History of
French Literature*, ed. by Denis Hollier, p.777), it must be
added that the novelist's unflinching representation of the harsh
realities of working-class life is in itself a considerable achievement and a protection against the distortions of biased, ideologically motivated glosses on (and glossings over) the sober
truths of his 'unvarnished tale'. *L'Assommoir* violated to extraordinary effect both the literary and the social proprieties of
his age. Not only are the characters and actions of Zola's novel
directed against the heroes and the plots of romantic literature,
but the novelist seeks, by the vividness of his narrative and
within the limitations of mimetic literature, to bring his comfortable readers into immediate contact with the misery of the
workers' conditions. We are to smell the stench of the slums,
hear the cries of hunger and anger of the starving, the 'silence
of the dying', the 'weeping women, the whining of starving
children, families tearing each other apart to try to forget their
hunger' (p.686). We are meant to see the dilapidated tenements,
the crumbling terraces, the layers of grime. We are led almost
to feel the searing pangs of hunger, taste the rotten scraps that
Gervaise is forced to scavenge like a dog, as she roams the
streets at the end of the novel, reflecting not only upon her
own wretched state but also upon the injustice of those who
would scorn her and the irony of her condition amid the signs
of prosperity around her:

Yes, she had been reduced to that; the idea was enough to disgust
refined people; but if refined people hadn't had a crumb to eat for
three days, we'd soon see if they'd ignore their bellies; they'd be down
on their knees eating garbage like anyone else. Oh, the starving poor,
their empty guts crying out of hunger, having to bare their teeth and
gobble up filth like animals, in this great, golden, shining city of
Paris!   (p.752)

Such passages are clearly directed at (or against) the bourgeois reader.

A common critical tendency in modern times is to devalue the referential and emphasise linguistic constructs and semantic ambiguities in realistic works. But the concentrated narrative strategies of *L'Assommoir*, its use of detailed 'scenes', its concrete description and, above all, its extensive use of popular speech all serve to draw even the most recalcitrant reader into complicity with its mimetic effects. With an unprecedented immediacy, Zola expertly evokes, along with the more horrifying scenes of suffering, brutality and deprivation, and such pathetic figures as old Bru and Lalie Bijard, the extraordinarily protracted disintegration of the Coupeau household. The grim daily necessities of an impoverished existence are vividly recorded: the search for food, the crushing debts, the desperate attachment to a few modest possessions, the threat of the pawn-shop, the 'shacking-up' (as opposed to bourgeois adultery), the promiscuities, the humiliations, as his characters sink deeper into the pitfalls of poverty. At the same time, Zola presents, within the limitations of his own vision, a total picture of popular attitudes and culture: the religious indifference, the gossip and the old wives' tales, the cheap, bungled ceremonies, the bric-à-brac on the mantelshelf, the constant moral compromises, the tenacious, unexamined prejudices and half-truths, the instinctive patriotism and, above all, the need for vicarious release, but not only in drink. Listening to the sentimental and escapist songs at Gervaise's feast, 'the men sat blissfully smoking their pipes, the ladies had a half-conscious smile of pleasure on their faces, they all imagined they were in some far-away place, breathing in delightful perfumes' (p. 587). Then there is the compelling desire to 'live it up a bit', all the more imperative as the situation deteriorates, in Breughelian scenes of unrestrained indulgence, all the 'grotesque realism' (in Bakhtin's expression) of bulging stomachs and stuffed orifices. 'It's true', the narrator notes in the same scene, 'you could see the bellies swelling up as they ate. The women looked as if they were in the club. They were all bulging out of their skins, the greedy lot! With their mouths wide-open and their chops all greasy, their faces looked just like backsides, and they were so red that you would have sworn they were rich folk's bums, bursting with prosperity' (p. 579). Such scenes are presented, not as evidence of working-class intemperance, but as gestures of defiance against the omnipresent threat of want and against the attitudes of the bourgeois reader, the implied narratee, as in the ironical views of the same revellers at Gervaise's party: 'There again, the worker, worn-out, penniless, treated like dirt by the bourgeois, had a lot to be cheerful about, and they come along blaming him when he has a drink or two now and then, just to brighten things up a bit!' (p. 579–80). In a general way, Zola has succeeded to a considerable extent, and certainly more than ever before in a major literary work, in not only evoking the desperate plight of the labouring classes, but also in depicting their culture in its vitality and specificity, which reformist homilies and political propaganda, with their own obtrusive, reductive view of the people, rarely take into account.

Thus the massiveness and intensity of Zola's mimetic achievement defies and problematises prepossessed and exclusive political interpretations. *L'Assommoir* cannot be wholly condemned as reactionary, nor praised as a progressive novel – it is a bold endeavour, but not a revolutionary work. It is too marked by and grounded in the prejudices of Zola's class and age to be a fully enlightened representation of the working-class condition. Yet, in a reactionary age, even a naturalistic description of social evils, if it is free from romantic idealisation, is a deeply disturbing, even seditious work. The class consciousness of the characters in the novel is not raised one iota, but the reader's could be, that is if the novel does not serve to confirm bourgeois prejudices against the working class. *L'Assommoir* shows the crushing burden of the workers' toil, even as it focuses on their idle dissipation. There are signs of the dehumanisation of the masses in the industrial age, an age which is not yet entirely past. 'Flesh', Goujet briefly intones in Hugolian fashion, as he watches a machine turning out rivets by the ton, 'could not struggle against iron. One day, of course, the machine would destroy the worker' (p. 537). But there are also passages in the novel (Goujet himself at his forge, Coupeau on the roof, Gervaise in her shop) in which the nobility of manual work is lyrically exalted. Zola's characters drink themselves into ruination, yet, before Coupeau's fall, his household is a model of industry, harmony, tenderness and propriety, which it takes, not the laws of heredity, environmental pressures, a wicked social system or the demon drink, but a mere accident to undermine. Zola's work, for all the rigour of its presentation and the systematic nature of its preparation, has more than the directedness of the sociological study, the political exposé or the moral tract. It has the indeterminacy and complexity of the novel. 'The novel or play as a structure, as a genre', David Caute writes, 'tends to *affirm* the individual and deny the society' (*The Illusion*, p. 81). As a novelist, Zola essentially deals with a unique individual's life, her plight, her struggles, her joys, her weaknesses and strengths, her 'problematic' situation within the dynamics of her group with its particular language and customs, not with the generalities of political argumentation or the categories of sociological investigation, the faceless 'masses' of the manifesto. Indeed, the 'tragedy' of Gervaise's fate, as we shall see, derives in large part from her loss of individuality and her lapse into a state of total anonymity. In short, *L'Assommoir* is not a dogmatic, programmatic text, but one which retains much of the openness of life itself and much of the ambiguity of literary art.

Chapter 2

The 'naturalist' novel

The family tree

Before going on to examine more directly the themes and techniques of *L'Assommoir*, we still need to relate the novel to Zola's naturalist aesthetics and to the second aspect of the scheme of the *Rougon-Macquart* series: the *natural* history of a family under the Second Empire. Without the class qualifier, Zola's definition of the subject of *L'Assommoir* in his preface to the novel, 'the fatal decline of a working-class family', could apply more generally to the whole of the *Rougon-Macquart* saga. The 'fatal' element is, as we have seen, largely socio-historical, but it is also, more appropriately, biological, invested in the laws of heredity as Zola and many of his contemporaries understood them: a fatal, disruptive force. There are very few happy combinations of genes, or, in terms more appropriate to Zola's age, few happy mixings of traits and dispositions in the *Rougon-Macquart*. Zola was drawn as much to the dramatic possibilities offered by the laws of heredity as to their scientific validity. They also provided the novelist with a framework and a further unifying theme for his series.

The early plans for the series contain detailed notes on Zola's main scientific source: an imposing study by Dr Prosper Lucas, dating from 1847–50, his *Traité de l'hérédité naturelle* (*Treatise on Natural Heredity*), in its short title. Zola would later update his information with some more recent theories when, in 1892, he came to write the final volume of the series, *Le Docteur Pascal* (1893), where the whole history of the family is recapitulated. He would note, for example, that the explanation given in *La Fortune des Rougon* and *L'Assommoir* for Gervaise's limp, namely the state of her parents at the very moment of conception, was no longer scientifically tenable (*RM* V, 1577). But, on the whole, as he wrote the series, the novelist put

Dr Lucas's treatise to constant use. He drew up genealogical trees and published them in 1878 and 1893. Each novel focuses on one or more of the members of this remarkable family, which is conveniently dispersed throughout the various strata of society. On the family trees, each member bears a label indicating, in the jargon of the day, the particular hereditary phenomenon that he or she represents.

The common stock is the neurotic Adélaïde Fouque, alias Tante Dide, who married Rougon in 1786, then, after her husband's death, took a lover, the drunken smuggler Macquart. Her children, Pierre Rougon, Ursule Macquart and Gervaise's father, the drunken Antoine Macquart, provide the three main branches of the family. The legitimate branch, issuing from Pierre Rougon's five children, is the most successful socially and politically, with a government minister (in *Son Excellence Eugène Rougon*), a doctor (in *Le Docteur Pascal* and elsewhere) and a high financier (in *La Curée* and *L'Argent*), along with a rather shadowy figure, Sidonie, with her shady business dealings. On this side of the family, the ruthless ambitiousness of the father tends to dominate. But the corrupt dynasty is condemned almost to die out when, symbolically, Aristide's grandchild, called (naturally) Charles, bleeds to death from haemophilia in the last novel, draining the tainted blood of the family away. Apart from Sidonie's lost and wayward child, Victor, from whom there is little to be expected, there does remain, however, the hope that a better future will be ushered in by the nameless child of the doctor, Pascal Rougon, who is remarkably free from the family curse, and his own niece, Clotilde (Aristide's second child), a union blessed with the full weight of Zola's lyrical approval, despite the warnings of Dr Lucas against consanguinary matching. The fifth child of Pierre Rougon, Marthe, marries into the middle (class) branch of the family, the Mourets, where the distaff side, with its neurotic female disorders, tends to prevail. Amongst Ursule's unfortunate progeny there is a headstrong revolutionary, Silvère, a neurotic priest, Serge (the abbé Mouret), a granddaughter, Jeanne, who dies young of a nervous affliction in *Une Page d'amour*, a mentally retarded granddaughter, Désirée, and a son, François Mouret, who goes mad (in *La Conquête de Plassans*). Yet here also there is a ray of hope, the enterprising Octave Mouret (of *Au Bonheur des dames*), who manages to inherit certain of his uncle's traits and marries a healthy shop-girl, Denise, producing two children, still too young at the end of the series to be 'classified' by the keeper of the family records, Dr Pascal.

But it is the other illegitimate branch, the Macquarts, that interests us most, the one which, as we would expect, is the least favoured socially and carries in its tainted blood the alcoholic strain from Antoine Macquart. But two of his three children, in fact, fare remarkably well. Lisa, in whom the mother's influence predominates, though hardly an admirable character, is stable and healthy in *Le Ventre de Paris*, as is her daughter, Pauline, in *La Joie de vivre*. Jean Macquart, the 'hero' of *La Terre* and *La Débâcle*, is by 1871 married to a healthy peasant woman and even becomes Zola's hope for the regeneration of France. But Gervaise and her progeniture turn out to be the most ill-fated members of the family. Of the children that we see in *L'Assommoir*, Nana will die horribly of smallpox soon after her son, Louis, after a hectic life as a courtesan; Etienne will be deported to Nouméa after the events of *Germinal* and the Commune (though he is reported to be married with children in New Caledonia); Claude, the un-balanced genius of a painter, will commit suicide in 1870 soon after the death of his own infant. A fourth child of Gervaise, Jacques Lantier, of whom there is no trace in *L'Assommoir*, will spring up to provide the homicidal train-driver of *La Bête humaine*. All in all, despite the hopeful signs and the positive tones of much of the narrator's discourse in the last novels of the series, the *Rougon-Macquart* novels present a cyclorama of disaster, which, in the space of little more than twenty narrative years, traces the rise, fall and, in many cases, destruction of so many members of this ill-fated family. No less than eight of the 32 remaining members of the family perish with the Second Empire in the years 1869–70. Five more of them are eliminated in the mop-up operation of *Le Docteur Pascal*.

The laws of heredity, interpreted as a fatal, destructive

force, play no small part in these chronicles of calamity and corruption. Yet, when one looks at the events of the novels individually rather than at what Zola and his surrogate narrators say about the series in passages of explanation, one finds that the scientific principles are not rigorously applied. *L'Assommoir* is, in fact, a good case in point. When she comes to Paris, as we read in both *La Fortune des Rougon* and *L'Assommoir*, Gervaise brings with her a heavy burden from the past. Back home in Plassans, her good-for-nothing, drunken father used to beat her and exploit her when she was old enough to work, just as he used to beat and exploit her mother, Fine. 'Conceived in drunkenness,' we read in the earlier novel, 'no doubt during one of those shameful nights when the couple would knock each other about ['s'assommaient'], she had a twisted and emaciated right thigh, a strange hereditary reproduction of the brutalities that her mother had to endure in an hour of furious fighting and drunkenness' (*RM* I, 124). This infirmity, which Coupeau gallantly overlooks (at least at the beginning of the novel) and which the Lorilleux cruelly mock, is the *stigma indelebile* of the hereditary destiny of Gervaise, born to a life of *assommage*, or, more precisely, the mark of her *mother*'s fate, which she is condemned to perpetuate, for there is a remarkable similarity between her own later situation, suffering at the hands of Coupeau and Lantier, and Fine's situation with old Macquart. She 'resembled her mother', we learn at the beginning of *L'Assommoir*, 'a hard-working woman, who died in harness and had been old Macquart's beast of burden for over twenty years' (p. 408). We learn also, in both novels, that Gervaise and her mother used to drink heavily, 'litres of anisette' (p. 417), to console themselves for their hard life and the brutality of old Macquart. Above all, Gervaise inherits her mother's sympathetic nature, her 'mania for getting attached to people' (p. 408). Zola sums up her character in his notes: 'A good-natured person, all in all; the reproduction of Fine.' In a similar way, she is defined in the 1878 version of the Rougon-Macquart genealogical tree in a laconic phrase (wrongly transcribed in the Pléiade edition): 'Representation of the mother at the moment of concept[ion].'

In the course of the novel, however, Gervaise seems largely to have shaken off her inherited or acquired propensity for drink. When we see her in chapter 2 with Coupeau in the Assommoir, she abstinently eats her plum and leaves the (alcoholic) juice, lecturing her future husband on the evils of drink. Apart from a tipple on festive occasions, she later continues to resist at least that particular temptation until the end of chapter 10, in circumstances that would have long driven a person with a purer pedigree to the bottle. Coupeau also has good reason to abstain: his father, a roofer too, had fallen to his death after drinking too much (p. 410). Only after a curious reversal of cause and effect has brought about the spectacular repetition of his father's fate (a fall leading to drink rather than the reverse), does Coupeau lapse into his bad ways. Even Goujet has a past to live down (with his mother's help): a drunken father, who, whilst under the influence, had killed a fellow-worker, then hanged himself in prison (p. 473). Zola is clearly protecting his characters from what he believed to be at least the immediate effects of hereditary drunkenness, to present a counter-argument to the easy association of the working class with alcoholic excess and to shift the responsibility on to social factors.

Yet, in the later novels, where there are several references back to the events of *L'Assommoir*, the explanation by reference to heredity is again foregrounded. In *Germinal*, for example, to explain his bouts of violence, Etienne Lantier refers to his 'drunken parents', who 'had put such filth into his body' (*RM* III, 1426). In *Le Docteur Pascal*, in particular, hereditary factors are blamed for Gervaise's children's woes (*RM* V, 1019). She herself is presented in this novel as the victim of 'the inevitable degeneration stemming from the milieu' (*RM* V, 1012), but she is also explained 'scientifically' as a case of direct hereditary influence from her father and even has a revised entry on the family tree (in the 1893 version) to that effect: '*Election* of the father. Conceived in drunkenness.' The jargon of Dr Lucas ('election') brings her fully back into the tainted lineage of the Macquarts, the offspring of the old soak, Antoine Macquart, who literally burns to death in this

same novel as a more symbolic than scientific case of sponta-
neous combustion, dying 'royally, like the prince of drunkards,
flaming up by himself, destroying himself in the flaming pyre
of his own body' (*RM* V, 1097). 'For all the prominence that
Zola gave to hereditary matters in his prefaces and genealogical
trees', Maurice Larkin notes, 'they make a somewhat lame
appearance in the novels themselves' (*Man and Society in Nineteenth-Century Realism* (London: Macmillan, 1977), p. 131).
Even Gervaise, 'despite her leg', as the narrator of the novel
would put it, becomes much more the prey of her new environment than the victim of her inherited characteristics.

The 'experimental' novel

Whether or not the weight of Zola's demonstration is towards
hereditary factors, as in *Le Docteur Pascal* and *La Bête
humaine*, or towards environmental influences, as is more
the case in *L'Assommoir*, both themes are characteristic of
naturalist literature. Here again, however, we find in the broader
context an even more pronounced disparity between theory
and practice. But a certain familiarity with Zola's aesthetic
principles is essential to an understanding of his works and
L'Assommoir is again a particularly significant case, since it
was precisely at the time of writing, publishing and defending
this novel that Zola gave the most forceful and elaborate expression to his naturalist tenets.

Naturalist literature is conventionally related to the broad
intellectual context of the tremendous prestige and influence
enjoyed by positivism and the natural sciences in what is
frequently termed the 'Age of Darwin'. Zola was, of course,
familiar with the theories of Auguste Comte and Charles
Darwin, but his principal mentor was the critic and art historian
Hippolyte Taine, who sought to apply the methods of the
natural sciences and a mechanistic or deterministic view of
human nature to the arts. Taine held the view that moral
and intellectual states can be as rigorously analysed as the
phenomena of the physical world and that physiology holds
the key to understanding human behaviour. He devised the

famous formula according to which 'race', 'milieu' and 'moment' are the determining factors that explain human behaviour. Zola's admiration for Taine dated back to the 1860s. A well-known dictum from his *History of English Literature*, which neatly sums up his views, was used by Zola as the epigraph to the second edition of his first 'scientific' novel, *Thérèse Raquin* (1868): 'Vice and virtue are products like vitriol and sugar.' In this novel Zola claimed to be studying 'temperaments' rather than 'characters', individuals ruled by their instincts, 'human beasts' ('des brutes humaines') rather than human beings. The novel traces the progress of the effects of animal passion, homicidal instincts and remorse in two adulterous lovers who kill the husband but are driven to suicide by psycho-physiological disorders. 'I have simply performed on two living beings', Zola claimed in his preface, 'the analytical task that surgeons perform on corpses.' The comparison between the writer and the doctor was already something of a commonplace of the time, as in the famous representation of Flaubert the surgeon, scalpel in hand, dissecting the hapless Madame Bovary. It was probably Taine's *History of English Literature* that put Zola on to Dr Prosper Lucas's authoritative and useful study of heredity.

It was at this time also, around 1866, that Zola began using the term 'naturalism', which he borrowed from Taine, to designate the literature of which he most approved. It was a convenient banner, deriving from a number of fields, notably the natural sciences, art criticism and philosophy, denoting the three disciplines from which literary naturalism emerged: a materialistic, even mechanistic philosophy, which subjects humankind to nature's deterministic laws, allied to a belief in the value of an empirical, scientific method of analysis applied even in the field of literature, along with the conviction that the novelist's art should attempt to achieve a faithful representation of contemporary life, even in its more sordid and trivial aspects, in opposition to the literature of the imagination, of moral edification, or of heroic and idealised actions in the classical and romantic traditions.

Zola's ideas did not really gain currency until after the

scandal of the publication of *L'Assommoir*, which, as we shall later see, gave momentum to the formation of a (brief) alliance amongst a group of naturalist writers and to a more lasting international literary movement. The furious debates over *L'Assommoir* also prompted Zola, in the late 1870s, to articulate his views more openly and more emphatically in a series of articles published in Russia and in France, which he collected together into no less than five volumes of critical studies that were issued in 1880–1 and that include his famous essay on the 'experimental novel'. There has always been a strong tendency to take Zola's ideas literally and to interpret his novels as products of his stated principles. It would be more accurate to reverse the terms and to interpret the theory as an attempt to justify more forcibly than before his firmly established literary practice in the face of hostile criticism. Zola's ideas belong very much to the context of the reception of his works, to a situation in which he was led to harden his views and express them with an intensity that immediately discredited them in the eyes of his contemporaries.

In 1879, Zola published, first in the Russian review *Vestnik Evropy* (in September), then in the Paris newspaper *Le Voltaire* (16–20 October), then again in his main collection of articles bearing the title of the offending essay, *Le Roman expérimental*, the article which caused most of the fuss. In 'The Experimental Novel', Zola took to extreme lengths the analogy between the tasks of the writer and the doctor, between literature and science, claiming that the two were virtually interchangeable activities. If Taine's ideas provided the inspiration (and the subtext) of Zola's essay, Claude Bernard's *Introduction to the Study of Experimental Medicine* (1865) provided, as well as a title, a battery of arguments and quotations that Zola used to full effect. Zola claims in this essay that the true novelist is both an observer who collects facts and establishes the grounds on which the demonstration that he is undertaking will unfold, and an experimenter who has his characters develop in a particular story according to the 'determinism of phenomena under scrutiny'. The novelist is applying scientific truths to the social sphere:

In short, the whole operation consists of taking facts in nature, then of studying those facts, acting upon them by modifying their circumstances and surroundings, without ever deviating from the laws of nature. The outcome is knowledge of man, scientific knowledge, in his individual and social actions.   (*OC* X, 1174)

Beneath the dubious theorising of Zola's essay can be discerned the need to establish, justify and bolster his belief that literature should be grounded in scientifically authenticated truths, rather than follow on from the imaginary schemes and moral imperatives that directed the romantic and moralistic literature that still held sway in France at the time. Zola sought to give a new, serious purpose to the novel. He overstated the case, for polemical purposes and for rhetorical effect (to give him the benefit of the doubt), for he was far less doctrinaire, especially when talking and writing to Flaubert, who privately dismissed his ideas as nonsense. Other critics did not hesitate to do so publicly.

The so-called scientifically verified laws on which, according to Zola, the 'experimental novel' should be based, and which were to be culled from medical sources and from the scientific theories that prompted them, did at least provide for naturalist works some essential features: guiding sequences of consequentiality and systems of probable, motivated development, a model of impersonal, dispassionate discourse on which to base realist fiction, as well as arguments to oppose to the attacks by moralists and traditionalists who shied away from the 'truth'. But only in a loose or metaphorical sense could one consider *L'Assommoir*, or any other naturalist novel, to be 'experimental'. As the traditionalist academic critic Ferdinand Brunetière dismissively and disdainfully argued in an article on the 'experimental novel' soon after the publication in France of Zola's essay, a novelist cannot perform an experiment whose outcome is unknown, since the writer is constantly in control of the results. To perform an experiment on Coupeau, Brunetière went on, one would have to find a real Coupeau, obtain exclusive rights over him, get him drunk each day with a measured dose of alcohol, then open him up to examine the results. If, however, Brunetière's cavils aside, one takes the association that Zola established between scientific experimentation and the novel more analogically than literally, if one recognises that the novelist can be guided by what he takes to be scientific knowledge in determining the outcome of the events of a plot by reference to probable causes and effects and if one bears in mind that, as Zola emphasised, the novelist is concerned, unlike the scientist, with the social consequences of physiological states, there are two ways in which a novel like *L'Assommoir* can be roughly termed 'experimental'. First, in the general ordering of the events of the novel, in the almost evidential way in which the novelist places his virtuous, principled character, with her acknowledged susceptibilities, and systematically submits her to a series of noxious influences that determine her decline. As we shall later see, the determinism is not as rigorously applied as Zola would have us believe, but, as the theatricality of the final scenes shows, there is an overall demonstrativeness in the presentation of the action of *L'Assommoir*, as there is in many novels which their authors would not dream of calling 'experimental'. In *Le Père Goriot* (1835), for example, Balzac places the noble young Eugène de Rastignac in the corrupt society of Paris during the Restoration and demonstrates his character's moral decline. Similarly, *Madame Bovary* (1857), to take another famous example, traces the effects of the stifling atmosphere of middle-class provincial life on a mettlesome young woman. Secondly, there is the manner in which Zola explains or hints at explanations concerning his characters' actions by reference to physiologically determining factors, to a sum of assumptions about human behaviour which 'motivate' these actions. The ambiguity of the term 'motivate' (to impel or, in the more modern sense of the word as it is often used by literary theorists, to provide a system of probable, convincing motives for human behaviour) raises the question of the scientific value of Zola's novels. The reader is left to wonder whether the novel exists primarily to illustrate certain established truths (however provisional they may be) about human behaviour, or whether the scientific explanations, explicit or implicit, are there merely to provide a convenient explanatory system, convincing enough to persuade readers to accept the dramatic, literary events of the novel as probable representations of the truth.

The 'case' of Gervaise nicely illustrates the question of motivation. We have already seen the limits of hereditary influences on this character who, for much of the novel, remains unaffected by the propensity to alcoholism that she supposedly carries in her blood. But there is in the character's constitution a physiological impulsion which is more discreetly presented in the novel and which, as it turns out, is more crucial to the plot: her physical attachment to her former lover, Lantier. When Virginie returns and first speaks about him in chapter 6, Gervaise experiences, we are told, a 'feeling of warmth in the pit of her stomach', an irresistible desire to know more about him, 'as if, suddenly, a gap in her life was being filled; her past was now running straight on into her present' (p. 549). She has the same extraordinary sensations later, feeling physically perturbed by the mere thought of Lantier. As the narrator explains, in significant metaphorical terms: 'She was thinking too much about him, she remained too full of him' (p. 600). This physiological version of lasting love is not in deference to the romantic tradition, but an implicit reference to a favourite Zola supposition. The 'impregnation theory', which is more fully illustrated in his early novel *Madeleine Férat* (1868), and which he may well have derived, initially at least, from reading Michelet's *L'Amour*, held that a woman retains the 'imprint' of her first lover even to the extent that her children by another man will inherit certain of his characteristics. When Nana is born, as her uncle Lorilleux observes, she does not look at all like her father: 'She was the image of her mother, with eyes from somewhere else; for certain, those eyes didn't come from the family' (p. 469). The discerning reader − though all this is unfortunately lost in the Penguin translation, where Nana's eyes are attributed to Gervaise (p. 113) − will remember at this point Lantier's striking eyes (p. 382). To confirm the 'fact', we read in *Le Docteur Pascal* that Nana 'resembled to an astonishing degree, especially in her childhood, Lantier, her mother's first lover, as if he had impregnated her for ever' (*RM* V, 1007). Gervaise's persistent attraction to Lantier and her subsequent submission to him are thereby explained 'scientifically', 'telegonically' (or, as we are more likely to conclude nowadays, pseudo-scientifically, mythically, patriarchally) by the 'fatalities of the flesh', as Zola had earlier called such irresistible impulsions. Yet, according to the information given to the Italian writer and journalist Edmondo De Amicis, on his working methods and on the genesis of *L'Assommoir*, the idea of having Lantier return came to Zola, in a flash of inspiration, quite late in his thinking about the novel (see L. Deffoux, *La Publication de 'L'Assommoir'*, pp. 30–1). The theory, then, provided a handy, 'motivating' explanation for Gervaise's reactions.

Rather than Gervaise, however, who develops in complexity and human interest as a character far beyond the limits imposed by her physiological condition, her daughter and her husband provide better examples of naturalist specimens. Nana is presented as a 'product' of her environment, as the plant and flower imagery constantly associated with her suggests. Most of chapter 11 narrates her 'education', thus supplying a lead into the novel *Nana* (1880), which will be exclusively devoted to her life, adventures and career as a prostitute and a courtesan. This gutter-snipe blooms in the filth of the slums and blossoms in the hot-house atmosphere of the workshop where, appropriately, she makes artificial flowers. She stems from the streets with all their corrupting ferment: 'She would stand still, pale with desire, and feel a warmth rise from the Paris pavements, creeping up her thighs, a ferocious appetite for the pleasures that she came across on the crowded streets' (p. 726). In *Nana*, she burgeons forth, taking on her full social significance (and again, somewhat too plausibly, her hereditary condition) in the article by the journalist, Fauchery, who presents her in particularly charged terms as the fatal woman, as the legendary 'Golden Fly', in his story of 'a young girl, born of four or five generations of drunkards, her blood spoilt by a long heredity of misery and drink, which was transformed within her into the nervous disorders of her female sex'. The article goes on:

She had grown up in a slum, on the streets of Paris; and, large, beautiful, with superb flesh like a plant gorging with manure, she avenged the beggars and the social cast-offs from whom she issued. With her, the corruption that was allowed to ferment in the people was rising and corrupting the aristocracy. She became a force of nature, a ferment of destruction, without wishing it herself, corrupting and disrupting Paris between her snowy thighs, making it turn sour, just as women, each month, turn the milk.   (*RM* II, 1269–70).

Clearly Fauchery's article is a device for introducing into the text the novelist's own interpretation of Nana's role. With its extraordinary mixture of metaphors, this passage illustrates the extraordinary mixture of science and myth in the novelist's art.

But, notwithstanding Brunetière's strictures, it is Coupeau rather than Nana who remains the most typically naturalist character of *L'Assommoir*, illustrating as he does a physiological condition before undergoing a transformation no less dramatic and mythical than that of his daughter. After a preliminary period of vitality, good health, devotion to Gervaise and pride in his skills, all abruptly brought to an end by his fall in chapter 4, the stages of Coupeau's decline are carefully charted as he lapses into idleness, drunkenness and madness. In true naturalist fashion, the emphasis is on physiological effects, but not entirely. Coupeau's reluctance to work seems to be prompted by a metaphysical sense of the injustice of fate. He bitterly bemoans his circumstances: 'It wasn't fair, his accident; it should never have happened to him, a good worker, neither an idler nor a drunkard. To others perhaps, he might have understood why.' His father had fallen off the roof when he was drunk, but, Coupeau complains, *he* was perfectly sober. 'If there *is* a God, he has a funny way of arranging things. I'll never swallow that' (p. 488). As he goes on to swallow limitless quantities of brandy, his questionings are subsequently buried in the prolonged binge that his life becomes, in mocking defiance of his fate. The symptoms of his moral and physical degeneration are clinically recorded as he is progressively transformed by the physical ravages of his disease into a grotesque 'sublime'. He acquires at first a perverse health and vitality, nourished by his excessive eating and drinking, all the time taking on an attitude of unrestrained mockery, becoming a kind of regressive human being, a curiously (and literally) *flamboyant* figure: 'His tousled pepper-and-salt hair was ablaze like a firebrand. His drunkard's face, with its ape-like jaw, took on a sallow hue and a purplish vinous tint' (p. 646). Zola derived much of the symptomatology of Coupeau's case from Dr Magnan's treatise, but his imagination took over, turning the character into a surrealistic figure, a burning vessel of alcohol, a 'combustible man'. Old Colombe's 'vitriol' takes its toll. Coupeau gives up eating, lives on brandy, becomes emaciated, starts to tremble, sniggers and grimaces all the time, until his whole system breaks down like a worn-out machine and he lapses into raving fits and hallucinations. In the Sainte-Anne asylum he becomes totally dehumanised, transformed into a jigging, puppet-like creature: 'That day, his legs were jumping about too, the trembling had moved down from his hands to his feet; a real punchinello he was, dangling on strings, his limbs hopping about, his body as stiff as a board. The disease was gradually taking over' (pp. 786–7). At the same time his body oozes sulphurous odours, for he is soaked in drink, reduced, as Gervaise will later be in the same chapter, but in a different way, to becoming the very substance of his condition, the 'fire-water' that he had consumed and that consumes him in turn. Images of fire and water fill his hallucinations. As Michel Serres notes, Coupeau's body turns into a still (*Zola*, p. 233). He ends in the horror of the outlandish contortions of the Saint Vitus's dance of *delirium tremens*, the syncopated chorea of his dipsomania.

Zola has clearly elaborated most imaginatively upon his sources in dramatising Coupeau's end, both taking up and deviating from the medical discourse of his age, as Naomi Schor has convincingly shown (*Les Cahiers naturalistes*, 52 (1978), p. 104). The basic manifestations of pathological intoxication are faithfully reproduced and coincide remarkably well with modern diagnoses of the links between alcoholism and mental disorders: the loss of appetite, the physical decline and, most dramatically, the paranoid attacks and the visual hallucinations in which patients believe themselves to be persecuted by plots, poisoning, torture, and see rats, dogs, colossal spiders and snakes — hallucinations that are close to the schizophrenic, but more intense, more externalised and more frequent. Though the symptoms of Coupeau's *delirium tremens* emerge when he is still on the bottle, Zola correctly depicts them with the greatest intensity at the stage of alcoholic withdrawal, when he is in hospital for his cures. However, the novelist's elaborations on the topic are revealing of the particular effects that he sought and of the significance, for him and his contemporaries, of Coupeau's state. Alcohol takes on an animate life of its own, becoming an insidious presence within the body. In Coupeau's first attack, we learn, 'the drink, which was lurking in his body, had taken advantage of the moment when his pneumonia had weakened him and laid him low, to attack him and twist his nerves out of gear' (p. 697). In his extreme state, Coupeau has visions of fairground festivities, of cascades of water and of flaming skies (pp. 783–4, 788); water seems to turn to brandy in his mouth (p. 787); he imagines a violent fight with Lantier and bloody mutilations of (presumably) his wife (p. 792). Building upon details in the rather sketchy notes that he had taken from Dr Magnan's book, Zola integrates them remarkably well (as we shall see later in the analysis of the themes and techniques of the novel) into the fabric of his text with its own intemperate developments: at a thematic level, in the interplay of elements and substances that form part of Coupeau's hallucinations; at the level of the plot, in the excessive, violent visions in which Lantier appears; at a mythical level, in Coupeau's carnivalesque delusions. But, above all, at a more discursive level, Zola's text remarkably represents the logic of excess of Coupeau's dementia, not only in the tale but also in the telling, as if the text itself were intoxicated by the syndrome, recreating the delirium of Coupeau's condition. These events are largely re-counted from the unstable perspective of Gervaise, using the free and easy style of the slang which, by the time we reach the final chapters of the novel, has taken on most of the narrative functions of the text. Hence the contrastive, corrective perspec-tive that is brought to the novel by the interventions of the medical staff at the asylum: the young house-physician who calmly takes notes on this 'interesting' case and impatiently dismisses Gervaise's questions (pp. 782–3), to be joined later by the elderly, weasel-faced specialist, with his titles, his penetrating look and his 'nasty, police inspector's manner' (p. 785). The medical staff provide, then, detached, objective perspectives on the scene: the moralist's disapprobation, the doctor's professional fascination, a fictive Dr Magnan with all his authority and authoritarianism, a 'decorated' representative of an institution which, the Foucauldian could argue with evidence from Zola's text, mirrors the whole repressive structure of the society in which it operates, defining and confining to preserve and protect its precarious order. Ultimately, these two characters also represent the naturalist writer – not the creator of a Gervaise, but the clinical analyst, the dissector (the *coupe-peau*) of Coupeau.

Naturalism

The progressive deterioration of 'character-specimens' into extreme states of madness, hysteria, homicidal mania, brutishness, physical and mental degradation, drunkenness, nymphomania, even lycanthropy, which release the beast in man (and woman) and push these characters beyond the pale of reason, order and integrity, is very much an essential part of naturalist thematics. Such themes, in their excessive manifestations, reflect a pathological vision of life, which the naturalist writers tended to share and which one of them at least, Maupassant, was condemned to live out when he lapsed into madness in an asylum in 1892. There is a significant disparity between the confident epistemology of (at least) certain naturalist writers such as Zola, Paul Alexis and Henry Céard, with their belief in the values of scientific investigation and realistic representation, and their deeper, more pessimistic ontological views, confirmed by their (somewhat partial) reading of the philosophy of Schopenhauer, as if the one were the dark side of the other. Nature for the naturalists in general was a lethal force, heredity a fatal curse, humanity the prey to biological urges, to irrepressible drives, to primeval impulses, and ultimately to the natural processes of degeneration and decay. In naturalist works there is a constant drift towards disintegration and dissipation, towards a loss of purpose, order and form. Lives are constantly wasted and energies spent. Moral and social structures disintegrate. There is a general levelling of values or a demotion of human beings to inhuman states. Naturalist literature is fundamentally ironic, exposing the gap between intention and achievement, between pretence and practice. Certain texts, like *Une vie* by Maupassant or *En ménage* (1881) by J.-K. Huysmans, merely portray the futile emptiness of a human existence in which hope is irretrievably eroded in the repetitive round of daily life and disillusionment becomes the essential experience as all events in life are reduced to the same plane of monotonous and purposeless banality. Others, like Strindberg's play *Miss Julie* (1888) or Hardy's novel *Tess of the d'Urbervilles* (1891), take up more dramatic models of action like the 'tragic' fall, precipitated (but more usually prolonged in time and due process as in *L'Assommoir*) by particular determining factors like hereditary defects or oppressive social conditions. In all, man – and, more often than not, woman, for woman is frequently presented in this misogynist discourse as the vehicle for disruptive natural forces – is submitted to a humiliating process of dehumanisation.

A generation of French naturalist writers, such as Paul Alexis, Henry Céard, Lucien Descaves and Léon Hennique, inspired by the works of Flaubert and the Goncourt brothers and by Zola's own novels, whose tendencies they often took to extreme lengths, fashioned a type of novel appropriate for these themes. More important than the reading of Claude Bernard for the development of Zola's fictional aesthetics was the example of the writers whom he considered to be (despite their protestations at being considered such) his naturalist forbears. Again it was at the time of the preparation of *L'Assommoir* that Zola was reflecting as intensely as in his earlier years on the art of the novel, as we see in the studies that he published in the Russian review, *Vestnik Evropy*, well before they appeared in France and well before he wrote 'The

Experimental Novel', notably his articles on the Goncourt brothers (September 1875) and on Flaubert (November 1875). Following the Goncourt brothers' example, he considered the word 'novel' to be inappropriate to the type of literature that he was advocating, with its implications of fantasy and fabrication. The major characteristics of the naturalist novel, he argues in the essay on Flaubert, are contrary to the novelistic tradition: the 'exact reproduction of life', the elimination of the hero and of heroic action, the eclipse of the author, who becomes the 'hidden director of the drama' (*OC* XI, 97–8). Flaubert set the standard, particularly with his *L'Education sentimentale* (1869), the drifting story of Frédéric Moreau's lost illusions and fruitless endeavours, for a type of anti-novel which, a generation later, the naturalist writers held in deep veneration. Zola described Flaubert's novel as the model naturalist text in the following terms (intended as complimentary): 'No one will go any further in depicting the real truth, I mean the down-to-earth, exact truth that seems to be the very negation of the art of the novelist' (*OC* CXII, 608). On the Goncourt novel (*Madame Gervaisais* in particular), he similarly wrote: 'This is no longer a novel in the proper sense of the term. This is a study of a woman, of a certain temperament, placed in a certain milieu' (*OC* XII, 172). The naturalist novel, Zola insists, disrupts the 'formula' of traditional novels with their complicated plots to become a study 'without peripeteia or dénouement, the analysis of a year's existence, the history of a passion, the biography of a character, notes taken from life and logically classified' (*OC* X, 1307–8). In the 1870s a new canon was emerging. Whilst *L'Education sentimentale* provided the exemplar of the apparently plotless novel of futile action, the Goncourts' *Germinie Lacerteux* (1864) established the more scientific model of the 'lesson in moral and physical anatomy', as Zola called it (*OC* XI, 170). This story of a servant woman who lives a secret life of drunkenness and promiscuity until her excesses lead to debt, illness and death, a work which their authors claimed in a resounding preface to be democratic in spirit by introducing the 'low classes' into the novel, presents, more than any of Zola's works (with the possible exception of

Thérèse Raquin), the standard naturalist clinical analysis. Dwelling upon the hysterical fits and the unbridled behaviour of its main character, *Germinie Lacerteux* presumes to present a case study, thoroughly and scientifically documented by reference to current medical theories, a depiction of neurotic female disorders presented in an assumed guise of scientific objectivity. It was a model text which Zola admired and which, to some degree, he imitated (though less than the jealous Edmond de Goncourt claimed) in *L'Assommoir*. But it was a type of work against which the younger novelist reacted in a negative way, as *L'Assommoir* also reveals.

In his theoretical and critical writings, therefore, Zola promoted the two types of fiction defined above: plotless novels recounting the disillusioning trivialities of everyday existence, and novels of catastrophic degeneration 'motivated' by scientific theories, two types which he insistently termed naturalist works and situated within the greater positivist tradition and in a lineage of writers stretching back to Balzac and beyond. In opposition to the literature of the romantic tradition, to the popular literature of illusion and distraction, and to the moralising literature which sought to consolidate the values of the prevailing order, the naturalist writers sought to represent life undisguisedly in its truthful aspects, however shocking or banal, with all the rigour and scrupulous concern for detail of the positivist historian or the scientific researcher. *L'Assommoir* obviously derives in some degree from these aims. Much of the novel describes the trivial realities of daily existence in a far from story-book setting and presents actions that are decidedly lacking in adventure. But Zola did not go as far in these directions as he might have gone or originally intended to go. In September 1875, he described his intentions for the novel to Paul Alexis: 'I have decided upon a very broad and simple tableau; I want banal effects with extraordinary facts, life in its day-to-day aspects.' At an even earlier stage, in the 1870s, according to the memoirs of Maurice Dreyfous, an associate of his publisher, Georges Charpentier, Zola had an even simpler plan in mind for the novel. *The Simple Life of Augustine Landois* would have been the story of a young laundress of impeccable habits and virtue, with a rigorous daily routine, who catches a cold one day, has coughing fits and dies soon after in the hospital, as work goes on at the laundry without her (*Ce qu'il me reste à dire*, pp. 1–6). Had the novel been written in this way, it would have been typical of a certain strain of naturalist fiction that relished the banal. In fact, Zola gave the name Augustine Landois to a minor character in *Le Ventre de Paris* and wrote with *L'Assommoir* a positively action-packed novel by comparison. It would have been even more so had Zola carried out a later plan, as we learn from the last section of his *ébauche*, to end *L'Assommoir* in the melodramatic key, with Gervaise, pregnant once again by Lantier, pouring (real) vitriol over her lover as he lies in bed with Virginie, then being dragged by him into the courtyard and kicked by Lorilleux as she dies and as Goujet and Lantier fight it out (*RM* II, 1545). The actual novel turns out to be a much more moderate compromise between the restraints of the naturalist aesthetic and the wilder promptings of Zola's imagination. There is a similar retraction from naturalist patterns in relation to the other type of text, the physiological analysis of human passions. *Germinie Lacerteux*, in its subject, setting, themes and preface, was clearly a model text for the author of *L'Assommoir*. But there is evidence that Zola resisted the influence of the Goncourts' novel in writing his own, not only by eliminating a number of similar scenes that he had planned to include, but also by making Gervaise less a naturalist specimen and more a rounded character with the result that she largely escapes naturalist, physiological typecasting, just as she largely escapes social stereotyping, as we saw in the previous chapter.

The scientific aims of Zola's *Rougon-Macquart* series and the naturalist aesthetics that he energetically developed to explain (and to justify) his works and the works of an emerging school of naturalist writers provide, therefore, important frames of reference for the interpretation of individual novels like *L'Assommoir*: a serious scientific purpose in tune with current medical research, objective and realistic descriptions of scenes from contemporary life, even in their more banal or hideous aspects. But, at the same time, we should recognise that Zola's theoretical and critical statements were frequently intended more for public consumption than for exegetic purposes, more as polemics than as poetics. They say very little, in fact, about the essential themes and techniques of naturalist works, remaining largely at a metadiscursive level. As Henri Mitterand points out, 'what is the source of much terminological and analytical confusion is that the naturalist *novel* ... and naturalist *discourse* are not homologous' (*Zola et le naturalisme*, p. 19). As the same critic and others have convincingly shown in studies of individual works – and as we have also seen in these two brief chapters – the genesis of a Zola novel brings into operation a complex set of factors. Along with the sociological and scientific facts, assumptions, methods and discourses, and together with the memories, observations, readings and plans, with all of which we have so far been mainly concerned, there were the previously unstated choices and procedures of the novelist's vision and craft, the profounder thematic patterns, myths, generic constraints, narrative models and technical innovations, a whole restructuring of experience of which only an intrinsic study of the novel, the main purpose of the following chapter, can give adequate representation.

Chapter 3

The novel: themes and techniques

In the labyrinth

Whereas French critics have been more inclined to study the character 'system' in the novel, critics writing in the English tradition, faithful to a long-standing assumption that the hallmark of great novel writing is the creation of characters, have emphasised the 'roundness' of Gervaise's character, the uniqueness of Zola's humble protagonist. Angus Wilson, for example, has described her as 'perhaps the most completely conceived character, belonging to that great class of submerged, unindividual figures that make up the very poor, to be found in all nineteenth-century fiction' (*Emile Zola*, p. 122). 'Neither good nor bad', 'in short, very likeable' ('sympathique'), are the terms with which Zola described his character in his preliminary notes. 'Gervaise is the most likeable and the most tender of the figures that I have yet created,' he wrote in his letter to *Le Bien public* (15 February 1877); 'she remains good to the very end.' *L'Assommoir* clearly conforms to the biographical tradition of the novel, as its first titles suggested, to the type of novel that traces the fortunes and misfortunes of a protagonist and engages the sympathy of readers, who see reflected in the character's failings the foibles of humanity, and sometimes their own. But Zola, with his characteristic sense of order, also instructed himself in his chapter plans: 'Divide my characters into good and bad.' A general study of the art of *L'Assommoir* must necessarily, therefore, begin with and focus on its main character, but must also constantly keep in view her function within the schemes of the work, its plot developments, its thematic, mythic and generic structures, as the key figure in the ordering principles of the novel and in the various parameters of its interpretation.

Such an approach allows us, initially at least, a coherent

view of the novel. It may seem unnecessary to labour this point, for, as many critics have pointed out, *L'Assommoir* is a work with a particularly rigorous scheme of development. With its rising and falling action, its carefully gradated progression, its skilful use of such devices as foreboding and retrospection to integrate the phases of the plot, Zola's novel appears to be a model of organic unity and coherence. But, in our age of suspicion of organised narrations and stable systems, we have come to recognise that the novel, even a work of acknowledged classical design, is both an open and a closed form. Whether or not we see it precisely, like a Lévi-Strauss, as a repository of disrupted myths that have lost their totalising power or, like a Bakhtin, as a meeting-place of various discourses, speech types and social voices, we need to be aware of the complexity, the capaciousness, the indeterminacy of the novel.

L'Assommoir, for all its directedness, leads the reader along diverse paths. Indeed, the image that most readily comes to mind to characterise Zola's novel is the maze, denoting both the entrapment of its main character, the inextricable dilemmas that she faces and that drive her ever further into her dire straits, and the remarkably patterned design of the work in which her destiny is played out. The maze suggests a double perspective: the confusion, the desperation and the plight of the victim trapped in the labyrinth *and* the privileged overview of the reader-onlooker who sees the pattern and admires aesthetically the devilish artistry of the construct. As Penelope Reed Doob points out, one of these perspectives is linear and temporal, the other architectural and spatial (*The Idea of the Labyrinth* (Ithaca: Cornell University Press, 1990), p. 1). The maze is a particularly suggestive image, one which combines, like all fundamental images in Bachelard's view, contradictory principles: order and chaos, clarity and confusion, unity and multiplicity, design and disarray. The maze is also a powerful mythical motif, associated with images and themes that are characteristic of *L'Assommoir*: lurking, monstrous figures, huge oppressive buildings, intimate refuges, guarded and threatened spaces, fatal descent, the loss of integrity of the self, the tyranny of time. A number of scenes in *L'Assommoir* directly evoke the image of the labyrinth. When Gervaise enters the huge tenement building for the first time in chapter 2, she enters a veritable maze of corridors in the very place where she will eventually lose her way and end her days. In chapter 3, the wedding party gets hopelessly lost in the maze of halls in the Louvre, and in chapter 6, when Gervaise visits Goujet's forge, she is caught in the industrial maze of the factory wasteland in the rue Marcadet. But there are also labyrinths of the mind, moral morasses, an irremediable loss of the self, irretrievable lapses into fatal errancy, which all apply to the destiny of Gervaise.

Gervaise

For all her centrality in the novel and for all the sympathy that she elicits from the reader, Gervaise's heroic stature is somewhat problematic. In the course of the novel she loses much of the moral superiority over her society that distinguished her in the early stages of the work. Her power, influence and prestige are progressively undermined and, progressively also, she loses the technical privilege afforded the heroic character of fiction, the dominant point of view on events, as her attitudes and language are assimilated with the collective voice of the society in which she fails to survive. Within the severely limited potentialities for success in her environment, hers is a story of riches to rags, a tale of the lady who literally becomes a tramp, the narrative of her physical and moral decline and fall.

There has been considerable interest, again mainly amongst English-speaking critics, in the question of Gervaise's moral decline. The moral development of his protagonist is skilfully 'motivated' by the novelist with a combination of the good, the bad and the indifferent at every stage of her progress so that the reader cannot attribute blame for her gradual downfall totally or exclusively to her weaknesses, or to the ill-will and wickedness of others, or to misfortune. This combination of eventualities is neatly summed up in one of the early expressions of Gervaise's ambitions:

Her dream was to live amongst honest folk, because bad company, she said, was like a bash on the head ['un coup d'assommoir'], it broke your skull and did for a woman in no time. When she thought of the future, she would break out into a cold sweat and compare herself to a coin tossed in the air coming down heads or tails depending on where it landed on the pavement. (p. 417)

In the opening scenes, Gervaise is all reason, wisdom and restraint, with her modest 'ideal', which she confides to Coupeau in the Assommoir and which will be periodically evoked in the novel as a marker of her fortunes:

Good Lord! I'm not ambitious, I don't expect much ... My ideal would be to get on quietly with my work, always have some bread to eat, have a decent little corner ['trou'] in which to sleep, you know, a bed, a table and two chairs, nothing more ... Oh, I would also like to bring up my children, make honest citizens of them if possible ... Then there's one more ideal, it would be not to be beaten if I ever took up with anyone again; no, I wouldn't like to be beaten ... And that's all, you see, that's all ... (pp. 410–11)

The outcome of the events of the novel will, of course, systematically undermine and reverse each one of these modest aims. Even in the early stages, Gervaise's weaknesses are noted, mainly her indulgence both with others and with herself, her 'unguarded moments'. When things go well, she develops a strong sense of property, a 'religion for her furniture', a particular cult for her clock, pride in her ownership of the shop, a confident, bourgeois dominance over her environment, as she almost bursts with prosperity like a character from *Le Ventre de Paris*. In the central phases of her development, a dynamic combination of factors and forces is brought into play: the outrageous ill-luck of Coupeau's fall, the debilitating effects on her will of the dirty laundry in the shop, her first 'spells of laziness' seemingly prompted directly by the 'asphyxiating' air of the shop, her excessive generosity to Coupeau, his drunken kiss 'amid the filth of her trade', which 'was like a first fall, in the slow degradation of their life' (p. 509). The gossips of the neighbourhood conspire against her, particularly the malevolent Lorilleux, whose malicious pleasure at her misfortunes is in a large measure instrumental in her decision to verreach herself by taking on the shop and by throwing her extravagant feast. Gervaise is shown to be the victim of that perverse, hypocritical and arbitrary power of gossips, who urge others to forms of behaviour of which they disapprove for the pleasure of blaming them later. Despite the salutary company of Goujet, whose uprightness and iron resolution strengthen her will, Gervaise's indulgences, her appetites, her pride, even her generosity, conspire to bring about the waning of her fortunes. Much of the novel – far more than one might expect – is taken up with the presentation of her wavering inner states, not in the manner of formal analysis, as in a psychological novel like Constant's *Adolphe*, but as what Zola called 'morality in action', a kind of applied psychology of which the stages and determinants are indicated by occasional discreet interventions by the narrator, or, more usually, in the character's own words through the medium of free indirect speech.

In the later phases of Gervaise's decline she lapses into a state of moral laxity, her resolution softened. A process of self-justification for her waywardness, a moral defence mechanism, enters into her attitudes: 'she defended herself, with so-called general reasons. When a woman had a drunkard for a husband, a dirty devil who lived in a state of filth, that woman could well be excused for seeking cleanliness elsewhere' (p. 637). The more idle and self-indulgent she becomes, the more she defers to the arbitrary rule of convenience, the very opposite of her earlier principles. She even thinks to exploit Goujet's kindness, an 'evil thought' (p. 669), to stave off some debts. She no longer cares when Coupeau is taken off to hospital, as she would have done before. 'Now Gervaise traipsed about, not caring a damn for anybody', letting herself go, neglecting her work, limping about in her degradation. 'Naturally', the narrator observes, reflecting the common view, 'when you get as shabby as that, all a woman's pride disappears' (p. 729).

The modern psychologist, a latter-day Dr Magnan in the field of moral development, would no doubt plot the stages of Gervaise's decline with the preciseness of the physiologist analysing the symptoms of *delirium tremens*. A Lawrence Kohlberg, for example, would see Gervaise regressing from what he would call a 'postconventional level of moral reasoning', the Kantian phase at which right and wrong are determined by reference to universal ethical principles, down to a 'preconventional level', the child-like phase in which they are determined by reward, punishment, power and expediency, with intermediary 'conventional' stages in which reference is made to societal standards and expectations. But, in a sense, Gervaise devolves beyond such a scale of values, to the ultimate 'natural' ethic: that is, into a pre-ethical state of complete moral relativism, in which anything goes and which is distinct from the moralising arbitrariness of those in the neighbourhood who criticise her. There is considerable sophistication in Zola's presentation of Gervaise's psychology of deprivation and desperation that is rare in literature, traditionally concerned with loftier inner struggles and more refined ethical dilemmas. There is, for instance, the character's despairing compulsion to spend which increases as her situation worsens, in defiance of the inevitable: 'it was as if she were intoxicated by the fury of running up debts; she lost her head, chose the most expensive things, gave in to her greediness now that she wasn't paying for anything' (p. 611). In this reversal of the bourgeois ethic, prosperity breeds economy and deprivation promotes a desperate desire to spend. Then, contrary to the bourgeois principle of the godliness of cleanliness, there is the luxury of filth in which she indulges: 'Even the dirt was a warm nest in which she took pleasure in snuggling.' A new household code, in praise of idleness and neglect, emerges: 'To let things go to rack and ruin, to wait for the dust to plug up all the holes and leave a velvety layer over everything, to feel the whole house heavy around one in a drowsy idleness, that was a real sensual delight that she fully enjoyed' (p. 644). There is also her total indifference to conventional values, which renders moral judgements irrelevant, belonging as they do to a world of ordered principles that no longer apply: 'Even the relationship between Lantier and Virginie left her totally unmoved, so indifferent had she become to all that nonsense that used to get her so worked up. She would have held the candle for them if they'd wanted her to' (p. 729). Like Coupeau's evolution into madness,

Gervaise's moral development takes her beyond conventional antinomies, beyond good and evil, into a state of moral indifference, equivalent, as we shall see, to her physical condition.

In a chapter of *The Moral and the Story*, Brian Nicholas presents a probing analysis of Gervaise's moral decline, illustrating the breakdown of her moral consciousness, her irresponsible neglect of Nana, her gradual adoption of the relative values of her society as 'natural', and her failing '*moral* ascendancy over her world'. However, surprisingly, the critic interprets *L'Assommoir* itself as a 'fragmentary and unsystematic plea for moral relativism' (p. 66), as a work whose challenge is to involve the reader dramatically 'in an action in which nothing is to disconcert or move us to moral reflection' (p. 67), a work which adopts a technique (narrating this action with the character's own voice) that retreats from any form of moral authority. 'The novel is a dramatized admission and demonstration', Nicholas writes, 'of the impossibility of an absolute moral judgment' (p. 77). But what appears in this analysis, with its nostalgia for the moral anchorage of the narrator's authoritative voice, as a weakness of the novel is precisely one of its strengths: the study of the limits of moral authority. Zola has demonstrated, not only that in oppressive circumstances moral principles waver and crumble, but that the very basis of morality is undermined. Morality is for those who can afford it.

The author of *L'Assommoir* has rightly been admired, not only because he was the first novelist to have a working woman as the central character of a novel, in defiance of the men of order, power, property, censorship and taste, who, according to Edmonde Charles-Roux, 'fear nothing more than having social inequalities denounced and their responsibilities publicly displayed', but also because Zola represented Gervaise not as a symbol, not as the 'Woman of the People' or Mother Courage, but as '*a* woman plain and simple, studied in all her complexity... This "heroine" is the opposite of a heroine' (*Les Cahiers naturalistes*, 52 (1978), pp. 10–11). Nevertheless, Gervaise has been appropriately compared to other well-known literary characters. Indeed, she has been linked to a whole series of naturalist heroines such as the Goncourt brothers' Germinie

Lacerteux and Renée Mauperin, Flaubert's Emma Bovary, Maupassant's Jeanne Le Perthuis, issuing from the naturalist mythology of woman as the perfect physiological being, the vulnerable victim of environmental influences, with her 'natural' propensities for nervous disorders, sensuality, even mystical folly. The most frequent comparisons are made, despite the differences of class and situation, between Gervaise and the heroine of *Madame Bovary*: the tendency to dream of a better life, the need to withdraw from an unsympathetic environment, the desire for immediate satisfactions, a certain vanity, sensuality and voluptuousness, a frantic need to spend extravagantly at the point of desperation. In the two novels, certain crucial scenes seem to have a similar privileged place and function in the curve of the protagonist's fortunes, notably Gervaise's feast and the 'comices agricoles' episode. But the most telling point of comparison is between the trilogy of 'lovers' in the two works: Charles and Coupeau, the husbands scorned, Léon and Goujet, the timid admirers, Rodolphe and Lantier, the ruthless seducers.

These analogies suggest a further, more technical sense in which Gervaise figures as the heroine of *L'Assommoir*, and of a further pointer to the systematic nature of the work. She is not only the central character of the action, but the central function in the character system of the novel. From a psychoanalytical perspective, there is the Freudian view that a novel's characters frequently reflect 'component egos'; from a structuralist perspective, characters derive their significance, not from their relationship to real-life figures, but from their role in the 'actantial matrix', in the structural model of the actions of the text. Gervaise's 'lovers', therefore, could be interpreted as expressions of the 'superego' (Goujet), her 'ego' (Coupeau) and her 'id' (Lantier), or at least, as we see in chapter 1 of Dubois's study, as levels of the heroine's personality: Lantier, of course, bringing to the fore, at the lowest level, her baser instincts, her irresistible physiological urges, which take over after his return; Coupeau, representing an intermediate stage, a mix of good and bad, potentially the agent of the realisation of her 'ideal', but, as it turns out, an agent of her decline;

finally, Goujet, her better self, all honesty, industry, probity, providing the source of inspiration in her early days and a measure of her degradation at the end.

But the associations do not end there, for other characters also appear as extensions of Gervaise's being and fate: old Bru, the prophetic thirteenth guest at her feast, who precedes her into abject misery, occupying the very hole under the stairs where she will end her days; Virginie, her rival, but a rival destined to follow in Gervaise's footsteps as she lives in the very same dwellings and becomes Lantier's next victim; old Bazouge, the undertaker, her last, grotesque 'lover', a symbolic figure of death, like the blind beggar in *Madame Bovary*, who finally satisfies her last wish; Lalie Bijard, an extreme reflection of her own martyrdom, of the batterings that she takes from life. Such systematic filiations fit into a broader spectrum of dynamic relations. On the one hand, there are associations that depend upon oppositions, on a Manichaean or melodramatic antithesis between good and bad, like the contrast between Goujet and Lantier, Hero and Traitor, relations which are reinforced in the dramatic phases of the action, in, for instance, the battle in the washhouse between Gervaise and Virginie (chapter 1), or in the bolt-making duel between Goujet and Bec-Salé (chapter 6). On the other hand, there are more mimetic relations, a proliferation of the same, which lead to a confusion of rôles, values, actions, and which tend to take over towards the end of the novel as differences are effaced and as Gervaise's struggle is lost: she joins the boozers, becomes like old Bru, takes on the speech of the neighbourhood gossips, imitates her husband's *delirium tremens*. To study more fully such significant effects we need to look more closely at the remarkably methodical structure and dynamic disposition of the plot.

Plot and structure

There has been almost unanimous acclaim amongst critics over the extraordinary feat of construction of the plot of *L'Assommoir*. They have expressed their admiration for the organic structure of the work, for the rigorous logic of its development, for the skilful use of 'scenes', narrative interludes, blocks of chapters, even to the extent of affirming, like Martin Turnell, that the novel's form is its redeeming feature. Henri Mitterand has also demonstrated that, in its stages of preparation, the novel underwent an exacting process of reordering and formal tightening, benefiting from the novelist's much-heralded sense of structure, from the architectural craftman ship which characterises all his works. The original plan of 21 chapters was trimmed to thirteen, a significant change, not only because it allowed the novelist to organise the plot with the new scheme in a symmetrical way, with six chapters before and after the central birthday celebration, but also because, as Gervaise reminds us in the same scene, it is the number of misfortune. This simple fact suggests that the rigorous formal arrangement of the work has more than a decorative function; it entangles and crushes the characters in its inexorable workings. This narrative model, as Henri Mitterand further observes, 'signifies, in the language of narrative structures, a fatalistic and pessimistic conception of working-class life, as at the same time it submits the enterprise of the social inquiry to the needs of tragedy' (*Le Regard et le signe*, p. 224).

The image of the labyrinth comes to mind again, in its more aesthetic aspects: the symmetry of its shape, the relatedness of its parts to the whole, the enclosed system that offers no escape, the specularity of many of its scenes. Certain episodes have been shown to mirror more general developments in the novel as a whole or to present ironic reversed images of fundamental situations. The visit to the Louvre becomes a *mise en abyme*, a mirroring of the whole text by a part of it, when the party gets enmeshed in the network of galleries and as their attention is caught by certain paintings (pp. 444–7) which reflect future tribulations (Géricault's *The Raft of the Medusa*), future carnivalesque revelries (Rubens's *Kermesse*), or, parodically, the miracle of Gervaise's feast(s) and her pathetic last supper with Goujet (Veronese's *Marriage at Cana*). To return to a more frequently analysed scene, which also occurs in the labyrinth, the bolt-making contest between Goujet and Bec-Salé in chapter 6 mirrors in miniature the fundamental struggles of the novel between the sober and the intemperate, the worker and the idler, healthy blood and tainted blood, rhythm and cacophony, order and chaos. Numerous other scenes (like the one examined at the end of this chapter) fulfil a similar reflexive function in relation to the totality of the work and lend themselves to detailed analysis. This is often true of minor details, like Gervaise's nightmare, an ironic reflection of her earlier dream, as she imagines herself at the edge of a well: 'Coupeau was pushing her with a punch, whilst Lantier was tickling her in the back to make her jump faster.' As she pointedly adds, 'it was just like her life' (p. 648).

The whole texture of *L'Assommoir* is closely held together by the tightly-knit interrelatedness of its parts, through anticipatory and retrospective devices, repetitions, sinister forebodings, ironic reminders. As Gervaise and Coupeau talk sensibly of marriage in chapter 2, ominous sounds are heard: the sobs of a drunkard lying in the middle of the street, the sound of a fiddle playing some ribald tune (p. 420). At the end of the same chapter, Gervaise looks up at the huge tenement building, which, menacingly, seems to be 'on top of her, its chilly mass crushing down on her shoulders' (p. 431). Later, old Bazouge, the undertaker, stumbles drunkenly into her wedding party (p. 462), a far from happy omen. Indeed, throughout the work there are constantly such reminders of the novel's finality: drunkenness, filth, deprivation and death. Chapters seem to follow a constant pattern of hope dashed in the face of reality, reflecting the general movement of the novel, or are framed by Gervaise's fears and premonitions, which will become her reality. Descriptions of her various lodgings recur, like the evocations of her hopes or the repeated appearances of Bazouge, in ironic iteration relating to her declining fortunes. In this novel repetition always takes an adverse turn, like the return of Lantier, on two occasions.

The fabric of *L'Assommoir* is thus made up of such carefully wrought effects and of such repercussions, as the hammer blows of the *assommoirs* constantly strike, all within a general pattern of measured gradation. The rhythm of the novel is of a relentless series of blows from which Gervaise is sent reeling (or limping), along with the more subtle and insidious worsening of her physical and moral situation. The plot follows a relentless rising and falling action in tune with Gervaise's fortunes, as this industrious, clean and abstemious woman attempts to assert her values but progressively lapses into idleness, filth and reckless indulgence. Work and activity are the dominant notes of chapter 1, as Gervaise, despite her setback, asserts her authority over her new environment and her prowess as a washerwoman; indeed, the whole chapter is a ritual cleansing, as Gervaise liquidates her past with Lantier. The exposition proper occupies the next two chapters, as Gervaise's moral creed ('I work, I am happy', p. 410) informs the whole section, imposing restraint on the wedding cele- brations, finding support in frequenting the upright Goujet household, with the squalor of the tenement building and the temptations of old Colombe's establishment kept at a safe distance. The rising action of the plot continues in the more dramatic phases of chapters 4 to 6; after the few years of hard work come the struggles against adversity: Coupeau's fall, his drinking, her first indulgences. But, essentially, in the first half of the novel, despite the baleful signs and the debili- tating effects of her work and her environment, Gervaise holds her own, purged of her evil appetites by Goujet's fire.

The birthday celebration, in chapter 7, is clearly the pivotal event of the novel, both the summit of Gervaise's success and the turning point in her fortunes. Indulgence replaces industry in the very workplace itself. In the euphoria of the occasion, Lantier is allowed back into her life. In more senses than one, Gervaise's goose is cooked in this peripety scene. In the follow- ing three chapters of desperate struggle (8 to 10), equivalent to the three that preceded the central scene, Gervaise enters the imbroglio of her fate in three decisive stages: in chapter 8, she is drawn to Lantier's bed; in chapter 9, she comes to accept, even to enjoy, the idleness and filth of her new condition; in chapter 10, she goes drinking in the Assommoir. Over this descending phase of her fortunes, the evil genie, Lantier, presides; Goujet, the solar figure, is significantly eclipsed.

The Coupeaus' dingy, sunless abode in chapter 10 is now the very antithesis of their bright apartment in chapter 4. In the final scene of this chapter, even the elements conspire against Gervaise, driving her into the Assommoir to seek refuge, where she comes face to face with the monster that will seal her doom, 'the still, the drink-machine, working away under the glass cover of the narrow courtyard, with the deep whirl of its devil's kitchen'. This infernal machine casts ominous, macabre shadows on the wall, creating 'obscene shapes, figures with tails, monsters opening their jaws as if to devour the whole world' (p. 704). After a drink or two she sees 'the machine move', feels 'its copper claws seize her'. She emerges, a spent force, staggering drunkenly into the filthy waters of the gutter. With cruel irony, the narrator adds: 'she thought she was at the washhouse' (p. 708).

The account of Nana's 'education' in chapter 11 serves to separate the phase of Gervaise's dramatic decline from the last two chapters of the novel, the coda of her misfortunes. The curve of her fate reaches its nadir in scenes which show the full extent of her degradation, like her desperate wanderings in the streets in chapter 12. She has become a shapeless shadow, a pathetic caricature of her former self, as she sees her reflection looming eerily out in the gas-lit streets: 'an enormous, squat and grotesque shadow, so round it was. It spread out, with its belly, breasts, hips all flowing and floating into one. She was limping so badly with her leg that the shadow on the ground tipped over at every step: a real clown she looked' (pp. 771–2). Now she wallows in filth, 'like a messy dog'; as she scrubs the floor in Virginie's shop, 'she looked like a heap of something not too clean on the floor' (p. 731). Her physical integrity has gone the way of her moral integrity. The brief final chapter, the epilogue of the work, where both Gervaise and Coupeau are finished off, is significantly anti-thetical to the prologue of chapter 1. There Gervaise had asserted her separateness from the environment and its contamination; here she is totally absorbed by her sordid surroundings, metaphorically eating dirt and literally eating filth 'to earn ten sous' (p. 795), then, as she is found already rotting in her hovel, *becoming* the filth itself, 'ça', a pile of the formless matter which she had spent the best part of her life seeking to eradicate and against which she had vainly sought to oppose her human values.

The structure of *L'Assommoir*, as this rapid survey indicates, follows a rigorous, symmetrical line of development, with a complex pattern of related elements integrated into a tightly structured framework. Though the events of the novel span several years, the seasonal settings of significant episodes also provide a coherent pattern: the novel opens in the spring; the central chapter, the summer solstice of Gervaise's fortunes, takes place at the end of June; most of the episodes that follow occur, with her decline, in the winter, with the last scenes set in the bitter cold and snow. The unities of the novel, then, its temporal ordering and the concentration of the action within a circumscribed location, along with its clear rising and falling action, seem fully to conform to the Aristotelian exigences of the classical plot. Critics have naturally tended to interpret the work according to this traditionally prestigious and authoritative model. R. M. Albérès even argues that one can be indifferent to the novel's subject, its character and its action, but there remains the fascination of a totally coherent work 'in which all the parts hang together like a perfect mechanism'. Zola's world, in this text, he adds, 'is a world that is full, without a flaw, without uncertainty' (*OC* III, 594–5).

But the reader should also be attentive to the gaps and the flaws, the inconsequentialities and the dissymmetries of even the most coherent of texts. One could equally well argue that, in fact, *L'Assommoir* develops, along roughly the systematic lines indicated above, from a state of structure and order into chaos and disorder at various levels of the text. The 'fullness' of the first half of the novel is undermined by the thematic disruptions of the second so that the formal framework becomes, in a sense, an empty, arbitrary structure. The latter half turns into a distorted mirror image of the former and the novel lapses, like its characters' conduct and language, into disorderliness. The novel becomes a kind of pit, as Jacques

Allard has suggested, with its falling actions and dizzying lapses, with the various 'holes' that Gervaise occupies in the progressively narrowing space at her disposal, with its cracks and fissures all around. The life of Gervaise, who lies prostrate in the opening and closing scenes of the novel, is clearly one long sequence of falls. She is drawn into a series of abysses, engulfing her and subverting the clear system of values of her ordered existence. Literally and figuratively, she finds herself 'in the hole', plagued by debt in the filthy hovel in which she must live. In the second half of the novel, like her Banban's foot, her whole life goes awry. The novel, in a sense, limps along with Gervaise's misfortunes, in a constant state of tipp(l)ing. The theme of claudication (limping) is ever present in L'Assommoir: Gervaise's fate is summed up by what she calls 'the misfortune of her leg' ('le malheur de sa jambe'); one of her sons is Claude; her husband breaks a leg in his fall and his first real binge is with Pied-de-Céleri, old Celery-Foot, a man with a wooden leg (p. 506). Time itself, in Gervaise's life, becomes out of joint. With great reluctance, she sells her pride and joy, the clock, symbol of the order to which she clings, the pendulum that, for a time, keeps her from the pit; but thereafter she loses her sense of time, time that is measured then by old Bazouge's grotesque cuckoo-clock. Even the neat and orderly clockmaker in the shop opposite Gervaise's laundry, a gentleman in a frock coat, for whom she has a particularly deep respect, goes wrong, almost brought before the magistrate for incest with his wayward daughter – an echo of the curious suggestion of a perverse relationship between her own daughter, Nana, and her lover, Lantier. In many similar ways, not only in its language, the second half of the novel is decidedly canted in relation to the first, 'the simple artfulness of the novel's structure', according to Roger Clark, 'seeking to mask the treacherous instability of an essentially anarchic world view' (*Zola: 'L'Assommoir'*, p. 47).

The apparent deterministic rigour with which the action of the novel is plotted can also be shown to disguise the gratuity of certain of its events. There are gaps in the causal chain of events in *L'Assommoir* that make a totally coherent reading impossible. What precisely causes Coupeau's fall, for which the text gives no explanation, even emphasising the roofer's skill at his job before the fateful event, 'always finding his balance' (p. 479)? Is the malevolence of the little old lady at the window, watching Coupeau work, 'as if she hoped to see him fall at any moment' (p. 480), reason enough? How do we explain Coupeau's radical change of character and what is Virginie's part in Gervaise's fall? In such cases the plot of the novel is motivated by mythical determinants more than by causal explanations, the myth of the Fall, Fate, the catastrophe of working-class life, evil forces at work. As we saw earlier, where Gervaise compares the uncertainty of her fate to the toss of a coin, pure chance plays its part. Hence, in old Colombe's Assommoir, another contraption that fascinates Gervaise: the wheel of fortune, the game of chance (p. 707). In such an ordered text, we see, in fact, how disorder and randomness play an inordinately significant rôle. We shall see, furthermore, in the following section, which deals with the themes and myths of this work, how disintegrating forms, shapeless matter, waste, filth, fluidity, come to prevail in the second half of the text and contribute to the dismantling of the systematic order of the world imposed by the first.

Themes and myths

The thematic richness of L'Assommoir is most aptly suggested by the multiple connotations of its title, for it is the novel of various assommoirs, if the meaning of the term is extended to include all those factors which come to oppress and overwhelm the victims of the novel. Close to the original meaning in the slang of the working class, it refers most literally to old Colombe's tavern and, by association, to all such places, to the strong drink that is fermented there and to the alcoholism that they foment. In a more generalised use of the term, it applies to all the evils of this society that drag Gervaise down, the oppressive milieu in which she lives, the city itself which demolishes her, the 'evil company' that she keeps, the brutality that afflicts her, the hereditary taints in her blood, the machines, monsters, nightmare visions that beset her, all that conspires to beat her down, destroy her spirit and finish her off.

From the start of the novel, the milieu in which Gervaise finds herself has a baleful presence, with frequent mention of the 'old slaughterhouses black with their killings and their stench', and 'the dreary new hospital, showing, through the gaping holes of its windows, stark rooms where death would wield its scythe' (p. 380). The tenement building, which will eventually swallow her up, is rotten and crumbling, with its grey inner walls, as 'bare as prison walls', its black shutters with their broken slats, its 'look of utter desolation' (p. 414). With the exception of the reprieve of her successful early years with Coupeau, Gervaise is trapped in a dark, dank, labyrinthine space, hemmed in by the city wall and closed horizon, moving in a colourless, clammy world of rotting forms. 'In fact, all the places that the young woman frequents are equally dangerous,' according to Colette Becker, 'all of them, including the beautiful blue shop. Brought to life, becoming like machine-monsters, they all secrete a damp and viscous atmosphere which weakens her and clings to her … All the places are traps whose characteristics are identical' (*Les Cahiers naturalistes*, 52 (1978), p. 49). Gervaise is thus mired in the miasma of her environment. This is indeed the central experience of her work too, her daily commerce with all the filthy laundry of the neighbourhood and its debilitating putrescence.

Zola's descriptions of this hostile environment, of these *assommoirs*, are more visionary than documentary, like his evocation of the monstrous still, which the drunkards worship in reverent meditation and which sends a shiver of fear down Gervaise's spine, tucked away in the shadows of the tavern: 'Quietly, without a flame, without a single spark of gaiety on its dull copper surfaces, the still went on, sweating out its flow of alcohol, like a slow but persistent spring, which would finally flood the room, spread to the outer boulevards, inundate the vast hole of Paris itself' (pp. 411–12). Coupeau becomes a devotee, filled, as we have seen, with the spirit of the still, a man-machine who comes home from hospital 'patched up and nailed together again … until the day when, laid up again, he needed a repair job once more' (p. 745). Bijard becomes a living bludgeon, an *assommoir*, beating to death his wife, a washerwoman like Gervaise, then his daughter too. The oppressiveness of the environment extends also to the sounds of the neighbourhood, where the bustling, reassuring cacophony of activity, hammers on anvils, ticking clocks and clicking irons, gives way to the deathly silence of despair, rent by cries of hunger and suffering. After the sunny days of success, Gervaise is plunged into the dark night of her misfortunes in the gloomy corridors of the tenement building and the dimly-lit streets. Even images of light and salvation take on an ironic force in Gervaise's darkest hours. 'The ugly mug of old Bazouge, with its twisted mouth and leathery skin thick with the dirt from all those burials, seemed to her beautiful and shining like a sun' (pp. 779–80).

Against the machinations of this malign environment the characters of *L'Assommoir*, particularly Gervaise, seek refuge, withdrawing rather than rebelling. As we see in Gervaise's 'ideal' ('a decent little corner in which to sleep'), it is not only the drinkers who take refuge in the snug. Against the threatening milieu, they seek a safe, intimate space: the warm laundry in winter, Goujet's forge, the Louvre, the warm glow in the Assommoir. Coupeau seeks refuge in the bottle. Lantier discovers his haven among the skirts in Gervaise's laundry, finding a more sensual version of her ideal: 'this whole little corner spot, just like an alcove, littered with the underwear of the neighbourhood ladies, seemed to him to be the nook ['trou'] of his dreams, a refuge of idleness and sensual pleasure that he had long been seeking' (p. 608). But, without Lantier's cunning, the characters of the novel see their refuges turn into *assommoirs* and are unable to resist their insidious influ- ences. The filth of the neighbourhood invades Gervaise's shop; the drink invades Coupeau's body. Whilst Lantier, we are told, 'eats' Gervaise, then Virginie, out of shop and home, the eating and drinking in this 'dog eat dog' world turns sour, like the general tenor of the birthday feast. *Consommer* becomes *assommer* and the characters are resorbed by the monstrous maw of their pernicious milieu. Only Goujet and the Lorilleux, the blacksmith-alchemist figures, who, whatever the differences in their moral qualities and their treatment of Gervaise, are associated and protected by their crafts, their links with gold, the *or* of the L*or*illeux and of Gueule d'*Or*, preserve the inviolability of the space that they occupy from the intrusive threat of the fire-water from the Assommoir or the foul corruption issuing from the milieu.

Beneath the surface of human actions and events, as these last comments suggest, a whole drama of the elements is played out in *L'Assommoir*. It is the novel of tainted sources, contaminated fluids, noxious liquids, that circulate in a world of fetid matter. Gervaise, whose fortunes are reflected in the colours of the waste run-off from the dyer's shop, is in constant contact with dirty water and ends up in the 'troubled' waters of the gutter. Coupeau, of course, works on the gutterings, dominating and directing this flow of dirty water, a privilege lost after his fall. Ironically, there are cascades and fountains of pure water in his hallucinations when the drink has already brought about his physical decomposition. If the wine flows freely at the feast, in the Assommoir the hard stuff sinks down into empty stomachs to perform its insidious task. The physical world of *L'Assommoir* is in constant dissolution from humidity, stagnant pools, grime, rust, rain, mud, dirty snow. Filth and the stench of decay are ever present, from the first scene, in which Lantier leaves behind symbolic stains in the sink, to the last scene of the novel. At this thematic level there is a clear association to be made between the fetid waters that invade from without and the poisonous liquids that destroy from within. Distillation, it is true, is a purification and the drink that the Assommoir dispenses is a means of transcendence over reality and over the corruption of the surrounding material world into the heady ecstasies of inebriation. But, as Coupeau's 'case' shows, in the inviolable economics that prevail in such resorts, there is the price of intoxication to pay. From the poetics of dissolution of *L'Assommoir* emerges a disturbing vision of a people who are the dregs of society, the bilge of the bourgeois world.

If one were to seek a more appropriate English title for this novel of stagnation and dissolution than those that it has borne so far in various translations (*Gervaise, The 'Assommoir', The Dram-Shop, The Gin Palace, Drink*), which denote a single aspect of the work, or more appropriate even than the one that Lilian R. Furst suggests, *The Club*, which could refer 'to both the place for drinking and the instrument for beating' like the French title (*'L'Assommoir'. A Working Woman's Life*, p. 29), one might suggest *The Sap*, a word with multiple meanings: a juice or fluid, body fluid, a foolish person, a trench or gutter, even a bludgeon, and various relevant cognate associations, with *sop* and *slop*, suggesting the various *assommoirs* that sap the will and drain the life from Zola's hapless characters. Ultimately, however, Zola's title evokes more than such diverse lineaments of the work. It connotes harsh, unbending reality itself, the law of reality that cannot be defied, circumstances and conditions more powerful than human will or desires. *La realidad es contundente.*

Myths and genres

In a work as richly suggestive as *L'Assommoir*, there are in-evitably complex mythical and generic associations which draw the reader out of the limited spectrum of the realist represen-tation of life in the rue de la Goutte d'Or during the Second Empire into the broader cultural context of fabulous figures and tales, of inherited conventions and forms, elements of which the novel, admirably suited for the purpose by its capaciousness, appropriates, adapts and transforms for its particular effects. There are, for example, undeniable biblical reminiscences in Gervaise's final descent into hell, in her last supper with Goujet, who shares his bread and wine with the fallen woman and gives her a last kiss. Her last, desperate walk through the streets in chapter 12, according to Roger Clark, 'takes us through the dif-ferent stations of Gervaise's calvary – the visit to the Lorilleux, the martyrdom of Lalie, the halts in front of Coupeau's atelier, of the hôtel Boncœur, of père Colombe's "Assommoir" – in an enclosed world that allows no escape' (*Zola: 'L'Assommoir'*, p. 48). The heroine's name, one could add along the same lines, refers back to the saint and martyr, Gervais, a figure of popular veneration in medieval times, whose saint's day, 19 June, is the date of Gervaise's feast. For the contemporary reader, no doubt, her name evoked the Pré-Saint-Gervais, the city gate with its hints of licentiousness and drunkenness. This mixture of the sacred and the profane — or, more precisely, the profanation and parodic demotion of the sacred and the prestigious by the profane, like the hope of salvation offered by old 'Colombe' (in French the 'dove') — is very much an integral part of the thematic fabric of the novel.

If indeed, as we have noted, labyrinths and monsters, the myth of the Minotaur, feature in this text, there are other mythical motifs that can be discerned. Goujet, to take the most obvious example, is clearly an exalted figure, exuding light, with his halo of blond hair, his pure traits, his Herculean strength:

A magnificent man at work, this fellow! The huge flame of the furnace shone fully on him. His short hair, curling around his brow, his fine yellow beard curling down, were all aglow, lighting up his whole face with golden threads — a real face of gold, without a word of a lie. What's more, a neck like a pillar, as white as a child's; a huge chest, wide enough for a woman to lie down on; sculptured shoulders and arms that looked as if they had been modelled on a giant's, in a museum... light radiating from him all around, he became beautiful, all-powerful, like a God.   (p. 533)

This larger-than-life figure, set in opposition to the ugly Bec-Salé with his 'goatee beard and wolfish eyes' (p. 532) and his awkward jerks 'like a monkey escaped from the zoo' (p. 534), a creature belonging to a lower order of life, recalls Hephaestus, the smith-god of classical lore, 'he who shines by day' (but without the limp). As for Gervaise's limp, a decided impediment in the naturalist world, it is a mark of distinction in the mythical order, linking her to a prestigious lineage of sacred figures and ancient fertility gods, evoking the primitive view (not entirely removed from Zola's 'science') that the feet are connected to the sources of vitality and that the maimed figure foreshadowed sterility and misfortune or, in the fertility sacrifices, the promise of plenty. Echoing Persephone's fate,

Gervaise's adventure is a descent into an underworld of sterility, suggested by her deep nostalgia for the countryside, her attachment to all forms of vegetation, like the tree opposite her window, the wallpaper in her shop, even the runner beans that she contemplates with regret, her 'dream of long ago', as she settles into her dingy new abode (p. 672). Lurking in their dark retreat, the Lorilleux have been described as chtonian creatures, like two spiteful gnomes, spinning their tales of vilification to destroy Gervaise and forging the symbolic chain of her fate, like sinister Parcae. Gervaise has even been compared to Eve, bitten by the serpent on the heel (a wound related to sexual intemperance), exercising a malefic spell over the aerial Coupeau, causing him to *fall* by her very look. The serpent in this fable is the still, with its snake-like forms, and it is in the lost paradise of the Assommoir, in its evil presence, where, in chapter 2, Gervaise bites into the plum ('prunes' denoting 'testicles' in the slang of the people), that the evil scenario begins ...

These elements of mythical figurations emerging from the sordid surroundings and vulgar action of Zola's work, with the ironic and travestied comparisons that they invite, give more than a hint of the generic complexity of *L'Assommoir*. The art of interpretation frequently consists of displacing a literary text from the context of conventions to which it has been familiarly assigned and of introducing it into a different exegetical frame of reference, without losing sight of the historical particularity of the text itself and, in the case of *L'Assommoir*, its ironic effects in relation to more prestigious generic conventions. Thus the famous battle in the washhouse in chapter 1, with its initial exchange of buckets of water as missiles, with the *corps à corps* that follows and the engagement with washing paddles that leads to Virginie's humiliating defeat, has all the makings of mock epic. The 'idyll' between Gervaise and Goujet culminates in the proposal scene of chapter 8, where Goujet suggests that they elope; the scene takes place in an appropriate 'natural' setting, on a patch of yellowed grass, under a dead tree, near to a tethered goat! He takes her hand: 'They didn't speak.' 'Up in the sky', the text goes on with strained pathetic fallacy, 'the flight of white clouds was swimming by with the stateliness of swans. In the corner of the field, the goat had turned to face them and was watching them, uttering at long and regular intervals a very soft bleating sound.' Their eyes are 'full of tenderness' as they gaze across the factory chimneys 'in the dingy and desolate district, where the bits of greenery by the seedy taverns moved them to tears' (pp. 615–16). The evident irony of this scene (and the ever-present taverns), leading to Gervaise's (not entirely 'motivated') refusal, betokens the text's own refusal of romance, its generic repudiation of the possibility of escape into adventure, of a bucolic solution. Just as Zola purposely restrained the urge to lapse into the excesses of melodrama and popular fiction, as we saw earlier, to enliven the darkest moments of his drama, he also held in check the romantic idealism that, if it had been more fully indulged, would have relieved the novel's dramatic tensions. In L'Assommoir, as is frequently the case in realist texts, its realistic effects derive in part from its subtle parody of the noble genres.

The noble genre which is most often invoked in commentaries on L'Assommoir is tragedy. Critics like R. M. Albérès have noted that L'Assommoir has the rigour of tragedy', a 'sense of a fatality which dominates great works', and that the novel may be defined precisely as a 'lay and popular tragedy' (OC V, 591–3). Whether or not one would adopt the view of a George Steiner that tragedy does not deal with secular dilemmas and that such a novel as this belongs to an age in which true tragedy is dead, or with the view of a Raymond Williams that tragedy is not the preserve of an élite, but part of the common experience, L'Assommoir clearly invites such consideration. The question is raised in the preface to Germinie Lacerteux, a work which, we know, influenced Zola's novel. There the Goncourt brothers asked if tragedy were, in fact, finally dead, if, 'in a society without castes and without a legal aristocracy, the sufferings of the humble and of the poor would awake interest, emotion, pity, as highly as the sufferings of the great and the rich; if, in a word, the tears that are shed below could make us weep like the tears that are shed on high'. We have already noted how the rigorous structure of Zola's plot, with its parabolic line of development following the rise and fall of Gervaise's fortunes, suggests the classical contours of tragic art. We have also noted how there exists an almost perfect symbiosis between Gervaise and the other characters, how the phases of her existence and her being are reflected in the lives of other characters, and how other characters, as in the economy of tragic drama, mirror the protagonist's fate. We could also observe that Gervaise's situation has the fatal imprint of the fundamental tragic situation, the dilemma, the aporia of the genre: a character condemned to do evil as he or she seeks to do good. Like Pentheus of *The Bacchae*, Gervaise is 'apt in [her] name to fall into misfortune', carrying the curse of heredity, that 'Nemesis without a mask', as Oscar Wilde called it. There is clearly a certain *hybris* in Gervaise's ambitions and an evident *harmartia* in the measures that she takes to realise them. Thus the action of *L'Assommoir* unfolds in that very gap which characterises tragedy: between human responsibility for evil and the inevitable order of things.

There is also much of the ritual expulsion, the fate of the scapegoat, to which tragedy in its anthropological sources is usually traced, in the destiny of Gervaise. She becomes a pariah, bearing, like the ritual model, the stigma of the evil to be expelled, a crippled *pharmakos*, regally fêted before sacrifice as the emissary victim in rituals of societal and cosmic renewal. Her links, mostly in the past, with the world of nature, the labyrinth into which she is drawn, the recurrent image of the spider's web (pp. 506, 528, 535, 643, 788, 791), the magico-religious aura surrounding the still, 'lit-up like a cathedral for a grand mass' (p. 769), and, in opposition to it, Goujet's forge, which fulfils the traditional rôle as a place of exorcism − all such fabular features confer a mythical, tragic dimension upon this humble tale. Goujet, the master of purifying fire, a civilising force, incarnating order, harmony and permanence, resistant to the degradation around him, is an Apollonian figure, whose luminosity radiates through the first half of the book. But the paean is transformed into a dithyramb as the opposing figure, Lantier, returns − the Dionysiac figure, incarnating the limping devil who draws out the dark, latent forces of

Gervaise's self. Her own gesture of exorcism ('she traced a cross in the air', p. 550) against Lantier's name proves to be ineffectual. Losing sight of the order of Apollo, she is dragged, like the Bacchae of old, into the excesses of Dionysos. The *nemesis* is long drawn out. Zola wrote in his *ébauche*: 'I have Gervaise die tragically, or rather I show her dying at forty-one, exhausted by work and misery.' The traditional tragic *topos* of violent retribution yields to the naturalist *topos* of a slow degradation.

With Gervaise's decline, the world around her undergoes a similar fate, as if, mythically, she were spreading her contamination to the whole of her society, rather than, realistically, being corrupted herself by her environment. The structures, laws, taboos, the whole system of organised differences on which a fragile social harmony is maintained, yield before the dissolution that overtakes this society. 'In tragedy,' Nietzsche wrote (in *The Birth of Tragedy*), 'civilisation is in a state of suspension.' This breakdown of order into dissoluteness, drunkenness, promiscuity, even incest, is heralded by Gervaise's feast. The occasion with which Gervaise sought to assert her distinctiveness, her power, inspired by the spirit of the *potlatch*, leads to a temporary abolition of all distinctions: 'Then, the whole society seemed to have melted away, some hiding behind others, all merging together, losing themselves in the dark streets of the neighbourhood, in a final uproar' (p. 595). In this veritable orgy, the 'binge spread, caught on from one person to the next so that the whole Goutte d'Or neighbourhood was sniffing the grub and holding its belly, in a devilish Bacchanalian orgy' (p. 581). In the lax spirit of indulgence, Lantier is admitted across the threshold into the order that is suspended, ready to bring about its ruin. With the feast the novel takes a turn for the worse, which prolongs its effects beyond the prescribed limits of the day, and the second half of the work becomes a carnivalesque, parodic reversal of the first.

In the phases of Gervaise's decline, along with the realistic descriptions of her terrible plight, the reader enters a bizarre world of degraded rituals. The more their real situation declines, the more the frenzied characters of the novel are impelled, in

evasion and in defiance, to eat, drink and be merry, before
the visit of Bazouge on the morrow. Every day becomes a feast
day, an occasion for celebration. 'They invented saints on the
calendar just to find excuses for a spree' (p. 558). In the carnival
spirit of the Assommoir, Mes-Bottes, in his worn-down shoes
and his dirty overalls, is proclaimed 'emperor of the boozers
and king of the hogs for having eaten a salad of live beetles and
bitten into a dead cat' (p. 622). Coupeau makes 'the drunkard's
sign of the cross. He pronounced Montpernasse on his head,
Menilmonte on his right shoulder, la Courtille on his left
shoulder, Bagnolet on his groin, and in the pit of his stomach
three times Fried Rabbit' (p. 627). Such outlandish parodying
of official institutions, beliefs, rituals, and discourses belongs
to the carnivalesque world that Bakhtin has so famously analysed. As the festive theme extends throughout the latter half
of the novel, the characters take on more and more grotesque
attributes. Coupeau is the prime example, with his vulgar,
blasphemous gestures, his farcical behaviour, his scatological
language, his giggles and grimaces: 'The roofer's mouth was
gaping so wide-open as he laughed that you could see right
down his throat' (p. 703). In his bouts of *delirium tremens*, he
becomes the perfect carnival figure, a man possessed, jigging
to the tune of his own destruction. This 'grotesque realism' is
the revenge of the body freed from all restraints: belly laughs,
bellies full, fleshy orifices, bloated shapes, unbridled indulgence,
in temporary relief from everyday constraints and interdictions.
But the characters of *L'Assommoir* seek to make it a permanent
state, a way of life. Like Mme Vigoureux at Gervaise's feast,
the more burlesque characters of the novel take on huge, shapeless proportions in a promiscuity of shapes and forms, even in
the face of starvation. Like her eerie shadow in the street light,
Gervaise becomes, as she scrubs Virginie's floor, 'a mass of
flabby flesh that shifted, rolled and jiggled about with the
jerky movements of the job' (pp. 731–2). The 'tragedy' of
L'Assommoir is played out in the life of the body of its
characters. In a first reading of the novel one is above all
sensitive to the catastrophic effects of the *assommoirs* on the
characters' lives, but a second reading makes one more aware

of the spirit of feasting and merriment so that the failures, miseries and sufferings of the characters almost seem to be secondary to what Jacques Dubois calls the 'great euphoric and explosive force that the novel contains' ('L'Assommoir' de Zola, p. 67).

Yet there is a profoundly sinister side to all this hilarity, which comes to affect even Gervaise, as she sits with Coupeau and his mates in the Assommoir, 'finally having a laugh as if she were being tickled and couldn't help it' (p. 705). There is a terrible irony in the festive mood of Zola's novel, a terrible gravity in his characters' levity, which is far from the frank and jovial frolics of the rural revellers of Rubens's *Kermesse*. The most carnivalesque figure of all is old Bazouge, the under-taker, who sums up in his person these grotesque tendencies: 'He was a real kill ['rigolo'], with a skinful every day and drunk out of his mind on Sundays, coughing and spitting and singing "Old Mother Godichon", uttering obscenities and fighting with the walls before finding his bed ... He was frightening, that creature, always laughing alone, as if his profession cheered him up' (p. 687). Gervaise's irresistible attraction for Bazouge is the dark, reverse side of her attach-ment to Goujet, as a juxtaposition of their names (Baz*ouge*-G*ouje*t) might suggest. This filthy, jolly drunkard is the messenger of *cras tibi*, the grotesque and mocking figure of the dance of death which dominates the final scenes of the novel, the grim japer who sums up the majestic symmetry of the simple tragic life of Gervaise, as he takes her away: 'Here's one that didn't want to, then wanted to ... Come on then, let's cheer-fully get on with it' (p. 796).

The carnival signals the victory of Dionysos over Apollo, the surrender to a vertiginous state that is essentially expressed in the dance. In *L'Assommoir*, the dance is a particularly significant theme. All the rhythmic movements associated with everything that is positive in the first half of the novel – the sun (p. 402), workers at their job (p. 416), Goujet's hammer (p. 533) – give way to the negative associations of the jigs and jinks of the second half: drunkenness (p. 695), death, the 'polka of deliverance' (p. 685), Bijard's brutality (p. 694), Nana's escapades, the hunger of Gervaise who has to 'dance in front of the cupboard' (p. 701) and, of course, the madness of her husband. Coupeau's crazy dance in the last chapter is described in carnivalesque terms, like a music-hall turn (p. 782). It is the dance of madness, transforming the character into a mechanical puppet, plunging him into a convulsive and fantastic dionysiacal rapture. It is also the dance of death, the stiff, gangling *danse macabre* of the corpses and skeletons in gruesome representations of doom. The theatricality of the action is particularly remarkable in Coupeau's performance, then again when the spirit of the dance is communicated to the fascinated gaze of Gervaise, who feels impelled to repeat the performance to amuse her neighbours. In this convulsive bacchanalian ecstasy from which there is no return, there is a total loss of the self. A fascinating mimesis occurs, a monstrous contagion that communicates and expresses itself in the bizarre contortions of the dance.

Language and technique

In a study of various familiar forms of French, *Le Français kiskose* (Paris: Fayard, 1975), Robert Beauvais notes that undertakers are particularly given to using slang to disguise the harsh realities of their work. The language of members of the professions that come into contact on a daily basis with the 'tragedies' of life takes on the most comical of expressions to 'dedramatise' their task. 'This verbal ritual serves as a safety valve. It exorcises misfortune by travestying it under grotesque masks and makes daily contact with it possible, contact which would be unbearable if those who are subjected to it agreed to see things as they are; it is a way of facing them better, in order not to see them' (pp. 6–7). One of the major functions of slang, one which clearly characterises much of the discourse of the latter half of *L'Assommoir*, is to serve this purpose. Old Bazouge's language is a perfect illustration of this need to euphemise the stark truth. His nickname, Bibi-la-Gaieté, makes the point and he is the one who provides the most startling example of the process, with the very last sentence of the novel, as he places the rotting corpse of Gervaise into her coffin with the words: 'Off to beddy-byes, my beauty!'

French novelists before Zola, such as Balzac, Hugo and Eugène Sue, had used popular speech in their works, but it was usually reserved for dialogues, set off from the narrative of the authorial voice and presented in italicised print to emphasise its quaintness and vividness, and its otherness. Zola's use of popular speech in *L'Assommoir* is significant and original not only for its extensiveness, but also because it becomes, as the novel progresses, the medium of narration, not merely quoted as discourse, but used with a narrative function. The idea of this technique, according to F. W. J. Hemmings (*Emile Zola*, p. 120), came to Zola in a flash of inspiration as he was waiting one day for a bus. It was a bold innovation, which provoked a strong critical reaction when the novel first appeared in serial form. In his preface to the volume the novelist responded to such criticism with a typically defensive argument:

My crime is to have had the literary curiosity to collect the language of the people and pour it into a finely worked mould. Ah! form, that is the great crime! Yet dictionaries of this language exist, literary people study it and enjoy its vigour, its unexpected and forceful images. It is a treat for linguistic researchers. Nevertheless, nobody has seen that my wish was to do a purely philological study which, I think, is of considerable historical and social interest.

It is true that Zola went about introducing popular speech into his novel in a systematic way. He borrowed words and expressions from *Le Sublime* and compiled lists of some 650 words from a dictionary of slang, Alfred Delvau's *Dictionnaire de la langue verte. Argots parisiens comparés* (1866), most of which he methodically ticked off and used as he went along. Many words and expressions in *L'Assommoir*, however, do not appear in these sources, for Zola was himself familiar with the language of the people, or, more accurately, the languages of the people, for the idiom that his characters use is a variegated compendium of several 'argots' merged in with more literary forms of expression. Thus the objection has been raised that the popular language of Zola's characters is not precisely or exclusively the idiom employed by the particular social group at the particular time represented in the novel. However, with time, the question of the authenticity of the slang of *L'Assommoir* becomes more and more academic, less a matter for verification or justification, as the discourse is perceived less and less (and more or less well) to *denote* the language of a particular group and comes to *connote* more and more the language and culture of the working class in general. Notwithstanding Zola's claim, the use to which he put popular speech in *L'Assommoir* is no more a 'philological study' than the novel is a scientific experiment.

If there is thus with time, as the geographical, historical and socio-economic context becomes more remote, a gain in apparent authenticity, there is a proportionate increase in difficulty for the reader and especially for the translator of a work which uses popular idiom extensively. Slang is notoriously difficult to translate, for it is especially subject to the flux of linguistic change and, like poetry, is a particularly expressive and metaphorical form of language. The translator of such a work is faced with a series of dilemmas: the choice, on the linguistic axis, between a literal rendering of the original style, which becomes comic and quaint, or a translation into the idiom of the translator's culture, with its concomitant departure from the source; the choice, on the cultural axis, between a translation that renders the particularities of the source culture, with direct borrowings for phenomena that do not exist in the target language, or a translation that transposes all such cultural references into a different context to create the illusion of a work issuing from the culture of the translator; finally, the choice, on the temporal axis, between a translation which attempts to reconstruct 'archaeologically' the idiom, local colour and temper of the age of the original text, or one which ignores historical development and simply uses the language of the translator's own age. Here, for a brief comparison, are four renderings of the sentence introducing Bec-Salé at the beginning of chapter 6, which reads as follows: 'Lui, se nommait Bec-Salé, dit Boit-sans-Soif, le lapin des lapins, un boulonnier du grand chic, qui arrosait son fer d'un litre de tord-boyaux par jour' (p. 530):

A The new-comer was called Salted-Chops, otherwise Drink-without-Thirst, a brick of bricks, and a dab hand at bolt forging, who wetted his iron every day with a pint and a half of bowel-twister (E.A. Vizetelly, ed., London, 1884).

B He was called Bec-Salé, otherwise Boit-sans-Soif, a bolt-maker of great dash, as strong as a horse, who rinsed his irons in a pint of brandy a day (Arthur Symons, London, 1895).

C He was known as 'Bec-Salé, alias Boit-sans-Soif', and was a bolt-maker of great strength and skill who always sprinkled his iron-forging with a bottle of rotgut per day (Atwood H. Townsend, New York, 1962).

D He was called Bec-Salé, alias Boit-sans-Soif, His Nibs himself, a star bolt-maker who lubricated his hammer with a bottle of fire-water a day (Leonard Tancock, Penguin, 1970).

Version A seems the least satisfactory by producing alien literal translations of the character's names and his drink. Version B is a marked improvement, but takes considerable liberties with the original, as does version C, which plays safe and produces a pale translation. Version D would, no doubt, be the best rendering for most modern readers, simply because, one suspects, its idiom, though already somewhat dated, is closest to our own. The art of translating a work like *L'Assommoir* compares in many ways to Zola's own task in writing the novel, moulding into a seemingly harmonious style a variety of registers of discourse. But the problem of translating Zola's text confirms the fact that the language of the novel is not just a philological exercise, but conveys cultural values and attitudes and has significant technical consequences for the novelist's narrative art.

Discussions of the technique of *L'Assommoir* usually centre upon Zola's attempt to achieve a homogeneous style by merging the literary discourse of the narrative with the popular idiom, the *écriture* of the 'bourgeois' writer with the *parole* of the people. This was very much a two-way process as Zola transposed passages of spoken language, usually its lexicon, into his narrative and adjusted popular speech to his narrative style. According to Marcel Cressot, Zola's feat fulfilled the novelist's claim (in his letter to Albert Millaud of 9 September 1876) to have achieved 'a uniform style', creating as he did it a 'new style which, harmoniously fusing the particular movements and tones of narrative with conversation, marks a date in the history of literary prose' ('La langue de *L'Assommoir*', p. 216). Faced with much the same problem as Flaubert, who wrestled with the need to write artistically with his characters' banal language, Zola, the standard view claims, devised a style that harmoniously blends disparate forms into a stylistic plenum. Zola achieved this effect, like Flaubert, with the device of free indirect speech, combining elements of the narrator's voice with oral characteristics, fusing the narrator's 'objective' narrative with the characters' 'subjective' discourse. In this mixed mode the punctuation signs of direct speech are suppressed, as are the enunciated formulas of indirect speech; the syntactical elements of straightforward narrative remain (the third person and the past tenses), but there are constant markers of oral discourse such as exclamations and questions. The result is a work in which different voices are supposedly fused to take on the narrative function: the narrator's, the characters', a collective voice. In general, the novel takes on a more oral tone, becoming less a story that the narrator narrates and more a story that the characters themselves seem to recount. More than 30 per cent of the text, according to calculations by Jacques Dubois, is in the spoken styles of direct speech (17.1 per cent) and free indirect speech (14.5 per cent). In many passages (like the one analysed below), the text shifts from one mode to another, through various intermediary stages. Edwin Grobe has defined six such modes: (1) 'bourgeois expository narration', the normal, Balzacian, narrative manner; (2) 'bourgeois dialogue transcription', where the characters' discourse is quoted; (3) 'proletarian expository narration', where the language of the people takes on the narrative function; (4) 'proletarian dialogue transcription', *indirect* discourse in the language of the people; (5) 'proletarian stream of consciousness', which recreates the subjective meditations of Gervaise; (6) 'proletarian proverbialisation', where the colloquial speech of the people issues moral generalisations, usually reducible to this simple example: 'Fortunately, you get used to everything in the end' (p. 648).

However useful and valid their distinctions, such analyses

have the disadvantage of presupposing that the style of *L'Assommoir* is, in fact, directed by a harmonious development. They tend to conflate distinct entities: levels of language, narrative modes, point of view. They fail to distinguish between the nature of the narrator and the sociolect of the speaker, or between narrative voice and the identity of the observer. 'Point of view' (the question of who sees what and why in a narrative), to take this aspect first, belongs to a particular order of narrative devices and has its variations. In *L'Assommoir* there is, for example, the surveying look, as in the opening pages of the novel, where Gervaise's gaze is used as a medium for setting the scene: 'And, with her eyes full of tears, she slowly looked around the miserable furnished room ...' (p. 375). Then there is the look of appraisal, a device for linking up elements of the plot, as Gervaise, later in the text, considers streets, buildings, familiar landmarks, that remind her and the reader of developments that have taken place. As she wanders in the streets of the neighbourhood in chapter 12, for example, she comes across the hotel where the novel began: 'She stood and looked at the first-floor window from which a torn sunblind was hanging, and she remembered her early days with Lantier, their first quarrels, the disgusting way he had left her' (p. 766). Various characters also act as witnesses to particularly shocking scenes, conveying their full impact to the reader: Gervaise's fall into adultery (seen by Nana, p. 633), into heavy drinking (seen by Lalie Bijard, p. 708), into prostitution (seen by Goujet, p. 774). Then there is the aggressive look, like the old woman's when Coupeau falls, or the scientific, searching gaze of the doctor in the asylum. In general, from the washhouse scene at the start of the novel to the dance performance at the end, there is a constancy in the way that Gervaise, a passive observer herself, is used and abused by the gaze of others.

But to return to questions of style and voice, by emphasising the transitional function of free indirect speech, critics have tended to convey the impression that *L'Assommoir* has a seamless style. But the different levels of language, the different styles of narration, the different voices, may also be seen as *contending* forms, with the language of the people, in particular, subverting the authority of authorial narration. The novel, as Bakhtin, chief amongst the theorists in this regard, has argued, is the genre of multiple *genera dicendi*, where different voices and different forms of speech interact. There is, for example, in *L'Assommoir*, a mode of writing that does not seem to partake of the main dialogic contrast between the 'bourgeois' language of the narrator and the popular speech of the characters (though marxist critics would unhesitatingly assign it to the former): it is the impressionistic descriptive style of several passages of the novel. In this drab, grey novel there are splashes of colour, intriguing effects of shadow and light, the 'golden dust of sunrise' (p. 377) that Gervaise sees from her window, Nana's pink dress, shining in the sunlight, her friend Pauline's white dress with its yellow flowers 'ablaze with little flecks of flame' (p. 712), in an impressionistic scene (the young girls walking arm in arm along the boulevards) that, in fact, Renoir sketched for the illustrated edition of the novel. In *L'Assommoir*, and even more so in other of his novels, Zola drew upon the subject matter common to writers and painters of the period, while artists such as Renoir, Manet and Degas drew inspiration from the novel. There are also technical links, as Zola adopts in certain descriptive passages (with considerable restraint, compared with the Goncourt brothers and their imitators) features of the *écriture artiste*, which disrupted the rational order of the classical style and instituted a more fluid perspective comparable to the visual experiments of contemporary painters. An impression of frenzied movement, for example, is rendered by an accumulation of participles and adjectives in descriptions of crowd scenes, as when, in chapter 1, Gervaise watches from her window the bustle of the start of a working day in the streets below: 'Then the office workers passed by, blowing on their fingers and eating their penny loaves whilst walking along; slim young men dressed in suits that were too small, with heavy, bleary, sleepy eyes; little old men with a toddling gait and faces pale and worn from long hours spent in their offices, looking at their watches to regulate their pace down to the last second' (pp. 379–80). Impersonal or weak verbal forms ('On...' or 'C'étaient...') and abstract nouns used for adjectives foreground the physical sensations that a particular scene conveys. In the washhouse, 'on respirait l'étouffement tiède des odeurs savonneuses' (p. 402) (literally: 'one breathed in the warm suffocation of the soapy odours'). In the courtyard of the tenement building, 'c'étaient des murailles grises, mangées d'une lèpre jaune, rayées de bavures par l'égouttement des toits, qui montaient toutes plates du pavé aux ardoises, sans une moulure' (p. 414) (literally: 'there were grey walls, eaten away by a yellow leprous scaling, streaked with drips from the guttering of the roofs, which rose straight up from the ground to the slates, without a single moulding'). Elsewhere, variations of colour and form are evoked in the changing light of day. As Coupeau and his helper work on the roof, for example, the 'sun was setting behind the building in a great flush of pink, slowly turning paler into a delicate lilac hue. And, across the sky, at this peaceful hour of the day, the huge silhouettes of the two workers stood out in the clear backcloth of the air, with the dark line of the bench and the strange outline of the bellows' (pp. 481−2). Such evocations and shifting effects of light and shape, this destabilisation of forms, and, similarly, the crowd scenes in which individuals merge into a general impression, though not a prevalent feature of L'Assommoir, add an alternative, more picturesque dimension to the styles of the novel − an alternative which, however, is only apparently dissociated from the two dominant modes of the text, the functional narrative and the character's rhetoric. Like the first, it presents, spatially as description, an equivalent drama of disappearing forms and structures; like the latter, it disguises the bleak and squalid realities that it aestheticises in a manner equivalent to the free and easy discourse of the revellers.

But there are other, more compelling ways in which the language of L'Assommoir disrupts rather than harmonises. Instead of merging with the narrative texture of the novel, the popular speech and free indirect speech perturb the course of the narrative, intervening, undermining and admitting an alien language and a deviating system of values, as if the struggle between the ethic of order and temperance and the ethos of indulgence, defiance and revelry were being played out at the discursive level. There is in the body of the text a constant foregrounding and backgrounding of popular language, of which it would take a sophisticated seismographic analysis to plot the variations. In the earlier stages of the progressive invasion of the novel by popular speech, the discordances are clearer, as in the following two consecutive sentences:

And, from time to time, in the middle of the sound of the irons and of the poker scraping the stove, a snore from Coupeau rolled out, with the regularity of the ticking of some huge clock, regulating the toil of the shop.

On the morning after his binges the roofer had a splitting headache, a terrible pain in his napper, so bad that he couldn't do his hair, his mouth tasted foul and his mug was all swollen and twisted.

(pp. 515–16)

It is as if the narrative takes on a tone appropriate to the behaviour of the characters or to their moral state. Zola can be admired for democratising the novel by writing about the people and using their language, but their language is still heavily charged with negative associations. It is introduced in spurts in the early stages of the work, mainly when Coupeau and the boozers (along with, noticeably, Virginie and Clémence) are described, often in mock religious terms. It remains the language of their degradation, in startling contrast, for example, to the direct, indirect and narrative discourse, worthy of the most conventional of novels, in the exchange of noble sentiments between Gervaise and Goujet in chapter 8 (pp. 614–17). It becomes more and more the language used to describe Gervaise as she declines. It takes on racy tones to describe Nana's burgeoning sexuality and the attentions of her 'admirer', 'a real groper, that one, pawing at her skirt from behind in the crowd, with an innocent look. And his legs! coalman's pegs, real matchsticks, they were' (p. 725). As we have already noted, it transforms into jollification even the most lugubrious of situations, like the scene in which (to return to the undertakers) they place Mme Coupeau in her coffin: 'Then, one, two, three, there we go! all four seized the body, two lifting by the feet, two by the head. As quick as tossing a pancake. The people craning their necks to see might have thought that Ma Coupeau had jumped into the box by herself' (p. 666).

Eventually, any clear distinction amongst the levels of style breaks down and a mixture of narrative voices takes over: the narrator's account, the narrator's adopted popular style, the narrator's ironic, mocking style turned against the people, the voices of the neighbourhood, of the drinkers, of Gervaise, all with their nuances of tone. Zola's remarkable feat of narration creates a promiscuity of styles, a babel, perfectly concomitant with the theme of the disintegration and the subversion of differences that we have seen to be essential to the novel. It explodes the hegemony of the conventional literary style of the novel and the discursive order from which it derives, the uniform realistic discourse which, normally unperturbed, fulfils its representative, historical, scientific functions. The vernacular style of *L'Assommoir* repudiates the very process of representation, opening up ironic gaps in the discourse, disturbing to the 'bourgeois reader'. At one level, this language exorcises the cruel realities which normally realist discourse simply describes, conveying, in a startling generic transformation, an extraordinary comic vision of the tragedy of Gervaise's life, which the wretched victim sums up herself as she reaches the end of her desperate walk in the snow: 'Then, as she climbed the six flights of stairs, she couldn't help laughing; an ugly cackle that hurt her. She remembered her ideal, from the old days: work in peace, always have bread to eat, have a decent place to sleep in, bring up her children well, not be beaten, die in her bed. No, truly, it was comical how it all turned out!' (p. 778). The ludicrous as a defence against the oppressive truth is a part of the ironic vision of the novel, for irony relativises everything and projects it outside the realm of prescriptive order into an egalitarian, Dionysian state of confusion. Thus Zola's novel presents both a representation and an ironic travesty of reality.

At the same time, the innovative, oral aspect of Zola's text, which transposes parts of it into a narrative spoken by the characters, has other far-reaching consequences. In addition to the two functions already defined, authentification and euphemisation, the popular discourse of *L'Assommoir* has an important pragmatic function. Slang is frequently a language of protest, the speech of the dispossessed and of the frustrated will, which devalorises and degrades the social conditions, the institutions and the circumstances that weigh down upon an alienated group. Its irony, blasphemy, insults, vulgarities, its colourful metaphors, are uttered and hurled in defiance of an oppressive order. It is the language of contention by the only means of reaction available, language itself. It is thus a defiance, a defilement and a denial of a situation of political powerlessness. The oral nature of the discourse (*discours*), which breaks down the barrier and distance between reader and event created by the objective narrative (*récit*) of a conventional, third-person, 'absent' narrator engages the reader in direct contact with this menacing effusion of words. This most effective mimesis, with the language of the novel imitating the language of its characters, replaces the reassuring, ordered scheme and narrative devices of the realistic novel, with immediate, disturbing effects.

The discursive style of *L'Assommoir* even achieves a certain dark lyricism, a crude dithyrambic effect, which appeals directly to the reader, capturing not only the rhetoric of protest, but also what the narrator calls the 'awful hymn of despair' (the 'sacrée musique du désespoir', p. 778) that resounds through the last chapters of the book. 'In the whole building,' the narrator observes on Gervaise's final abode, 'a great lamentation arose. Weeping could be heard on every floor, the music of misfortune droned along the corridors and the staircases' (p. 683). Exploiting the resources of this rich and vivid language, Zola introduces his own poetic rhythms to give voice to his characters' lamentations and to give free rein to their expressive idiom. The language of the people and the rhythm of Zola's prose style combine to create the effect of what Jacques Dubois calls 'a kind of immense song'. A particular narrative rhythm emerges, about which, according to Dubois, 'one can scarcely speak in terms of action or plot'; indeed, 'the narrative in the classical sense breaks down' (*'L'Assommoir' de Zola*, pp. 182–3). The language of *L'Assommoir* takes on an intoxicating euphony of despair and of delirium; it is distilled into a heady discourse, a verbiage of excess, folly and despair, beyond which lurks the dark inarticulate state of death. Coupeau is reduced to the silent language of his body in the last throes of his agony, Gervaise to a defeated mutism in the last months of her life. The ultimate *assommoir* is that non-discursive reality, that implacable fate which the drink of the Assommoir and the language of *L'Assommoir* can never dispel.

Gervaise's day

One of the most impressive episodes of *L'Assommoir*, which has been widely admired, as a moving evocation of the despair of Gervaise, as a technical accomplishment in its use of free indirect speech and as a recapitulation of the novel, occupies the whole of chapter 12. This winter's night, her mind befuddled by hunger, losing track of time, Gervaise is seen first lying on the straw in their filthy, desolate hovel, waiting for Coupeau to return, as she had waited for Lantier in the opening scene. Then she embarks upon a desperate tramp back and forth along the very streets that, in that same scene, she had surveyed from her window, between the hospital and the abattoirs, revisiting in her plight all the sites of her misfortunes: 'It was her last walk, from the bloody yards where the slaughtering went on ['où l'on assommait'], to the dingy wards where death laid out the stiffs in communal sheets. Her whole life had taken place there' (p. 771). She begs from the Lorilleux, witnesses the death of Lalie Bijard, is pushed into prostitution by Coupeau, limps along in the snow, meets old Bru, then Goujet, who feeds her, then begs old Bazouge to satisfy her last dream: 'a corner of greenery in the Père-Lachaise cemetery' (p. 779). The technique of concentration of time and point of view in this episode, its extensive use of interior monologue, has led critics to compare it to Joyce's *Ulysses*, with its ambulatory hero and its prostrate heroine, Molly Bloom. Though more ordered than the stream of consciousness of the later work, the 'tragic' soliloquy of Gervaise does flow freely as she is caught in the maze of streets and in the white labyrinth of snow, and as she traipses in the cold, the wind and the darkness of the despair, in a funereal twilight zone of shadow and shapeless forms, where she sees

her grotesque reflection in the dull lamplight and hears lugubrious groans drifting through the night. The whole climate of
the poetics of death, or of the approach of death, is evoked in
this scene, which leads inevitably to the threshold of Bazouge's
door.

The tally of her life's misfortunes is most impressively
illustrated by the following passage, in which, like a Beckett
character, Gervaise pathetically looks back over her 'happy
days':

Ah! oui, Gervaise avait fini sa journée! Elle était plus éreintée que
tout ce peuple de travailleurs, dont le passage venait de la secouer.
Elle pouvait se coucher là et crever, car le travail ne voulait plus
d'elle, et elle avait assez peiné dans son existence, pour dire: 'A qui
le tour? moi, j'en ai ma claque!' Tout le monde mangeait, à cette
heure. C'était bien la fin, le soleil avait soufflé sa chandelle, la nuit
serait longue. Mon Dieu! s'étendre à son aise et ne plus se relever,
penser qu'on a remisé ses outils pour toujours et qu'on fera la vache
éternellement! Voilà qui est bon, après s'être esquintée pendant vingt
ans! Et Gervaise, dans les crampes qui lui tordaient l'estomac, pensait
malgré elle aux jours de fête, aux gueuletons et aux rigolades de sa
vie. Une fois surtout, par un froid de chien, un jeudi de la mi-carême,
elle avait joliment nocé. Elle était bien gentille, blonde et fraîche, en
ce temps-là. Son lavoir, rue Neuve, l'avait nommée reine, malgré sa
jambe. Alors, on s'est baladé sur les boulevards, dans des chars ornés
de verdure, au milieu du beau monde qui la reluquait joliment. Des
messieurs mettaient leurs lorgnons comme pour une vraie reine. Puis,
le soir, on avait fichu un balthazar à tout casser, et jusqu'au jour on
avait joué des guiboles. Reine, oui, reine! avec une couronne et une
écharpe, pendant vingt-quatre heures, deux fois le tour du cadran!
Et, alourdie, dans les tortures de sa faim, elle regardait par terre,
comme si elle eût cherché le ruisseau où elle avait laissé choir sa
majesté tombée.   (pp. 767–8)

(Ah! yes, Gervaise had finished her day too! She was more worn out
than that whole crowd of workers who had just gone pushing by her.
She could just lie down there and peg out, for work no longer had
any use for her, and she had toiled enough in her life to be able to say:
'Who's next? As for me, I'm done for!' Everybody else was eating
now. It was the end, the sun had snuffed out its candle, it would be
a long night. Oh God! to stretch out comfortably and never get up
again, to think that you've put away your tools for good and can
put your feet up for all eternity! Just the job, after twenty years of
knocking yourself out! And Gervaise, her stomach racked by the pangs

of hunger, couldn't help thinking back to the days of feasting, to the nosh-ups and good times in her life. There was that time especially when it was bitter cold, one Thursday in the middle of Lent, when she'd really lived it up. In those days she was really nice, blond and fresh. Her washhouse in the rue Neuve had named her carnival queen, in spite of her leg. Then they'd gone gallivanting along the boulevards in carts decked out with greenery, right in the middle of all those fancy folk that really looked her up and down! There were all them gents that put on their monocles like she was a real queen. Then, that night, they'd had one hell of a nosh and danced about till they dropped, right through till the dawn. A queen, she'd been, yes a queen! with a crown and a sash, for twenty-four hours, twice round the clock! And now, weighed down, in the agonies of her hunger, she looked at the ground as if searching for the gutter into which she had let her former majesty fall.)

This paragraph sums up the whole of Gervaise's adventure in a chapter which fulfils the same microcosmic function, reviewing the essential phases of the heroine's story. It also contains at the beginning a snippet of direct speech ('A qui le tour? moi, j'en ai ma claque!') that, on a smaller scale, provides a further and ultimate summary of her fate. The passage also typifies the extensive use of free indirect speech in the later stages of the novel. The two sentences beginning with an 'Et' ('Et Gervaise, dans les crampes...' and 'Et, alourdie...'), which triggers the shift in mode, two sentences which frame the reminiscence, are attributable to the narrator's discourse, containing elements of popular lexicon in the first, the 'nosh-ups' ('gueuletons') and the 'good times' ('rigolades'), and the effective literary flourish of the cadence in the second ('où elle avait laissé choir sa majesté tombée'), which conveys the impact of the character's fall into the gutter. The rest of the paragraph belongs to the intermediary mode that links the character's inner discourse with the narrative account of her reflections. Gervaise thinks, but the narrator records her thoughts: 'C'était bien la fin, le soleil avait soufflé sa chandelle, la nuit serait longue.' The exclamations ('Ah! oui', 'Mon Dieu!', 'Voilà qui') are the most evident signs of the character's actual thought, whilst the tenses ('pouvait', 'voulait', 'avait peiné'), the third-person pronouns ('elle', 'se') and Gervaise's own name maintain the discourse within the control of the narrator's voice.

The divisions of the paragraph express the contrasting reactions of the character to her plight, the two dominant tones that we have defined in the novel. In the first half of the paragraph, which ends at 'pendant vingt ans', the free indirect speech captures the grim and muted lyricism of the starving woman's lament. The second half, which projects her out of the harsh reality of the present, recreates, again in muted tones, the jaunty strains of revelry that characterise so much of the latter part of the novel, until the inevitable rude awakening, the coming down to earth of the final sentence.

This paragraph neatly epitomises the novel at a thematic level, with its insistence on the motif of the fall into abject misery, with its carnivalesque theme and with its synecdochic condensation of Gervaise's life into the events of a single day. Like her life, 'her *day*' ('journée') is a simple but key element of the text. It is the day's work that denotes her past toils and her present idleness. It is the 'day' of glory and success, as the passage later makes clear, the day that even every dog has, and her 'day' that she has *had* now that all is lost. It is the 'day' that she has lost in her battle with all the enemies that oppress her and the symbolic 'day' of light that is irretrievably lost as she is plunged into her darkest hours. It suggests the 'day' of life, soon to come to an end, now that the candle is out, the 'days' of her youth, strength and vigour, now irretrievably lost except in the imagination, also her 'day' in both precise terms (her fateful birthday celebration of chapter 7) and, more generally, her 'day', her age, her time, her past, which, in the gloss of retrospection, is always better than the present.

To these social, existential, thematic, symbolic, narratological connotations must be added the tragic time-frame of the fate of this fallen heroine, 'twice round the clock', the rising and setting of the sun of her fortunes. The event that Gervaise recalls thus reintroduces in summary form themes related to the carnivalised tragedy that is *L'Assommoir*: the mock-religious celebration (in Lent), the mock-queen, the unrestrained festivities, the parade, even the vegetation decorating this humble *kore*, with the hints of a parodic apotheosis, the appurtenances of her glory days, the crown and the sash − all this 'despite her leg', the ever-present reminder of her tragic flaw. We see too in this passage the defiance of middle-class prosperity, respectability and tyranny by the revellers, as Gervaise recalls with pleasure how she could 'épater les bourgeois', shock the 'fancy folk' and the 'gentlemen' in a moment of sweet revenge. But this passage is also remarkable in being not only a review of the novel, but the account of an event which occurs nowhere in the preceding narrative. It is thus literally a 'paragraph', a para-story, a turn that the narrative might have taken, all the more revealing symbolically for its absence in the actual story of her life. It could be interpreted, then, as wishful thinking, a *day*-dream, a product of Gervaise's distraught mind, like the hallucinations of her husband, here a euphoric denial, as is so often the case in this work, of the reality of her condition. But, as ever, that reality, the *assommoir*, is not to be denied. The key theme of the fall and the key motif of the prostrate woman prevail. No longer erect and proud, she is a fallen queen, 'flat out', ready to 'just lie down there and peg out', 'to stretch out' and never to rise again, bludgeoned into submission, down in the element of her destiny and of her degradation, the filthy stream of the gutter.

Chapter 4

Repercussions

The usual way, though not by any means necessarily the best way, to measure the success and to judge the impact of a literary work in the immediate context of its publication is to examine the reactions of critics. Their opinions, reflecting rival interests and ideologies, are invariably divided and, very often, the louder their protestations, the more acerbic their criticism, the more likely the work proves to be a lasting success. We have already looked at the revealing division of opinion amongst critics on political grounds. Less significant and more pre-dictable were the expressions of moral outrage that the novel provoked, though if they reveal little about the qualities or faults of the novel, they reveal much about official standards of the age. If should be remembered that, until June 1877, the year of publication of *L'Assommoir*, the French Republic was still largely under monarchist control, and 'the moral order' was very much the order of the day. La Fontaine's tales and Casanova's memoirs had recently been banned. The writers in vogue were the tepid, moralistic Victor Cherbuliez and Octave Feuillet. Thus violent protests of indignation from conservative critics were hardly surprising. Albert Millaud, in *Le Figaro* of 1 September 1876, denounced Zola's novel even before its publication was complete: 'It is not realism, it is smut; it is not crudity, it is pornography.' For B. de Fourcauld, writing in *Le Gaulois* of 21 September, it was the most complete collection that he had ever known of 'base acts without any atonement, qualification, shame'. The venerable Catholic critic, Armand de Pontmartin, denounced the novel's 'abominable licentious-ness' in the *Gazette de France* (18 February 1877), whilst, in Henry Houssaye's estimation (in the *Journal des Débats* of 14 March), *L'Assommoir* belonged to the realm of pathology rather than of literature.

However, the novel was not without its defenders, even in the conservative press. Albert Wolff disagreed with his colleague (in *Le Figaro* of 5 February 1877) in his evaluation of Zola's 'remarkable book'. But it was mainly left to fellow-writers, either in public statements or private letters, to define the qualities and originality of the novel. Anatole France called it a 'powerful book' (in *Le Temps* of 27 June 1877) and defended Zola's use of popular language. Paul Bourget (in a letter of 2 February 1877) argued that the fury of the critics' attacks was proof that *L'Assommoir* was Zola's best novel, his most original work. 'You have invented a style', he wrote. 'It is troubling like all discoveries, upsetting so many received ideas that one must be daring to admire you just as you have been daring in writing.' More traditional realists, like Champfleury, had reservations about Zola's audacities. Flaubert, the master stylist, when he read the serial version of the work, accused Zola, in his correspondence, of becoming a *précieuse* in reverse, but he later warmed to the novel's overall powerful effects. A no less exacting writer, Mallarmé, in a long letter of 3 February 1877 which defies literary categorisation, expressed, with more than a hint of irony, his profound admiration for Zola's 'great work', a work 'worthy of an age in which truth has become the popular form of beauty!' But his praise was thoroughly sincere as he added: 'You have endowed literature with something absolutely new, these tranquil pages which turn like the days of a life.'

It was, in fact, the publication of *L'Assommoir* in France that prompted another important statement by a poet, Swinburne. This was the first significant comment by an English critic on Zola's works, though, with his taste for drink and the 'birchen mysteries', Swinburne was hardly the most appropriate spokesman for public morality to denounce Zola's novel. But inveigh he did against the novel in *The Athenaeum* (16 June 1877): a 'loathsome' work, in his view, containing passages that 'deal with physical matters which might almost have turned the stomach of Dean Swift', a work which, he acknowledges, he could not bring himself to read in its entirety. Thus began, from this most unlikely source, the campaign of moralistic denunciation of Zola's works in England that would eventually lead to the imprisonment of his English publisher, Henry Vizetelly, in 1889. But in other quarters the novel inspired different reactions. George Moore, a francophile living in France, was converted to naturalism by reading Zola's novel and sought, with limited success, to institute an English naturalist movement. Indeed, it is hardly an exaggeration to claim that, in the politics of literature, *L'Assommoir* was a revolutionary work. In the 'quarrel' surrounding its publication in France, a group of young writers rallied to Zola's defence. Guy de Maupassant admired the novel's 'prodigious power'. J.-K. Huysmans wrote laudatory articles in a Belgian review. Léon Hennique scandalised the literary establishment by pronouncing the superiority of the author of *L'Assommoir* over Victor Hugo in a controversial lecture on 23 January 1877. With Paul Alexis and Henry Céard, these novelists and short-story writers fêted their elders, Flaubert, Edmond de Goncourt and Zola, a few days after the publication of *L'Assommoir*, in the much publicised gathering (called the 'dîner Trapp') at a Paris restaurant on 16 April 1877, an event which supposedly marked the founding of the naturalist school of writers. They also formed the so-called 'Médan group', who published, along with Zola, the famous collection of short stories, *Les Soirées de Médan* (1880), a work heralded by literary historians as the manifesto of the school. As with all such literary events, there was as much advertising as substance involved in the claims that this inaugural dinner and publication were manifestations of the existence of a vigorous new literary movement, but the rallying of this group of young writers around the beleaguered author of *L'Assommoir* and their defence of his novel were undeniably important factors in contributing to a certain unity of purpose and agreement amongst the naturalist writers, much more so than any adherence to the novelist's own theories. Zola's influential novel has a prominent place in the history of nineteenth-century French literature and its impact abroad was no less significant.

Zola's novel deserves to rank as a landmark of *world* literature for its far-ranging influence beyond the borders of

France both as an individual text and as one of the principal naturalist works that inspired naturalist movements or tendencies in numerous countries not only in Europe but throughout the world. It was in fact in the immediate aftermath of the publication of *L'Assommoir* and of the heated debates to which the novel gave rise that Zola's influence and, with it, the spread of naturalism really took hold. Evidence of the impact of Zola's influence abroad is contained in the multi-volume edition of his correspondence, where one sees how, quite dramatically, in the late 1870s and early 1880s, Médan became a centre of attraction on an international scale. There were constant enquiries from abroad, expressions of admiration and even of discipleship, contracts with foreign publishers to negotiate and protests against pirated editions to be made, requests for contributions and interviews from foreign periodicals, pleas for prefaces from aspiring writers. By the time *Nana* (1880) and *Pot-Bouille* (1882) had added their own scandalous effects, along with the publication of the novelist's controversial theoretical studies on naturalism and the 'experimental novel', Zola's works and ideas were being debated and imitated as vigorously in other countries as they were in France. By the end of the 1880s, when the novelist's French disciples had largely abandoned him, when he himself was questioning his own naturalist methods and beliefs and when French critics were solemnly announcing the death of naturalism, Zola's works and ideas were still gaining currency outside France.

In his study of the spread of naturalism in various European literatures in the last century (in *Le Naturalisme*, 1982), the French comparatist Yves Chevrel, with the usual proviso about the artificiality of schemes of periodisation, discerns three distinct phases of development that occurred after an initial period in the 1860s that saw the publication of a small number of naturalist works in France such as *Thérèse Raquin* (1867) and Flaubert's *L'Education sentimentale* (1869). In this scheme, *L'Assommoir*, still a relatively isolated text in the 1870s, was clearly a pivotal work, for the first 'ground swell' of naturalist literature arose from 1879 to 1881 with texts by Zola and his followers in France largely dominating the picture but with a number of foreign writers – Fontane in Germany, Capuana in Italy, Ibsen in Norway, Strindberg in Sweden, Pérez Galdós and Pardo Bazán in Spain – producing naturalist texts. The 'high tide' of naturalist production was, according to Chevrel, the period from 1885 to 1888, when examples of naturalist works appeared in every European country, particularly in Germany, with the early years of the 1890s producing a last 'wave' that added a number of American texts to the European corpus. As individual studies of Zola's influence show, there were in most countries common campaigns of resistance by traditionalist critics, a common flood of translations and adaptations of the novelist's works, followed by a spate of novels, short stories and plays inspired by the French writer. There was frequently an active, progressive intermediary campaigning on Zola's behalf such as Michael Georg Conrad in Germany, George Moore in Britain, Jan ten Brink in Holland. But there were also significant variations in the reactions to Zola's influence.

In the 1870s, even before the publication of *L'Assommoir* had brought Zola such notoriety in France, his works were well known in Russia, mainly by virtue of his contributions to *Vestnik Evropy* and the serial publication of his novels in Russian journals, appealing as they did to the liberal middle-class readers and the radical socialists of the country. Zola's influence in central Europe was channelled partly through his Russian connections to such influential literary periodicals as the Polish *Przegląd Tygodniowy*. *L'Assommoir* and other *Rougon-Macquart* novels naturally influenced practising novelists abroad, but in Germany, to take another exceptional case, where Zola counted prominent admirers like Conrad, Karl Bleibtreu and Conrad Alberti, there was also much theoretical discussion on naturalist principles, on the relationship between science and art, on the question of morality in literature – indeed far more discussion of this kind than in France. There also emerged in Germany, as in Scandinavia with the plays of Ibsen and Strindberg, a significant concentration on the theatre, particularly in Berlin where Arno Holz, Gerhart Hauptmann and Hermann Sudermann produced naturalist drama with more success than their naturalist counterparts in France.

But Zola's influence was particularly marked in Latin countries, no more so than in Latin America, where Eugenio Cambaceres, Javier de Viaña and Carlos Reyles were amongst his most ardent admirers. In Italy the publication of *L'Assommoir* met with instant enthusiasm and success, for the novel was widely read in the original French and in rival translations (by Petrocchi and Rocco). In a famous study, 'Zola e *L'Assommoir*' (1879), the eminent Italian critic Francesco De Sanctis expressed reservations about Zola's 'system', but more liberal critics like Felice Cameroni were unreserved in their praise and an article on *L'Assommoir* by the Sicilian writer Giovanni Verga (in the *Corriere della Sera* of 11 March 1877) is considered to be one of the founding texts of the *verismo* movement, the Italian variant of naturalism. In Spain more direct influences by *L'Assommoir* can be traced. The novel by José María de Pereda, with its imposing title *Don Gonzalo González de la Gonzalera* (1879), for example, took up the theme of drink and the working classes, as did the plays of Joaquín Dicenta, *Juan José* (1885), and Leopoldo Alas ('Clarín'), *Teresa* (1895). In December 1883, theatregoers in Madrid saw an adaptation of *L'Assommoir* called *La Taberna* by Mariano Pina Domínguez, a hastily composed piece in which, as in other adaptations elsewhere under different names, the heroine, Gervasia, and Juana (Nana) are saved from the treachery of Virginia and Germán (Lantier) by the brave Nicolás (Goujet). More discreet signs of the influence of *L'Assommoir* can be found in more prestigious Spanish texts such as *Flor de Mayo* (1895) by Blasco Ibáñez (the Spanish novelist most closely associated with Zola's influence), where a troublesome lover's return and a fight between two women in a fishmarket echo scenes in Zola's novel. But more significant perhaps than such incidental borrowings is the recurrence in a number of works of the more general theme of the decline and fall of a woman (usually of humble origins) for which *L'Assommoir* provided the model: in *Giacinta* (1879) by Capuana, *La Tribuna* (1883) by Emilia Pardo Bazán, or *O primo Bazilio* by the Portuguese writer Eça de Queirós.

In Britain and the United States, Zola's influence met with

considerable opposition from moralists and public authorities. *L'Assommoir* was presented to the English-speaking public, to use the expression of the anonymous reviewer of the *Literary World* (21 June 1879) about one translation, in a 'deodorised' form, all language and scenes likely to give offence having been carefully expunged. But the French novelist had his admirers and imitators such as Theodore Dreiser, who was often referred to as the 'American Zola', and Frank Norris, who referred to himself as 'boy-Zola'. In the latter's *Vandover and the Brute* (1914), the hysterical fits of Vandover, called his *lycanthropy-mathesis*, have been compared to Coupeau's bouts of *delirium tremens*, and his final humiliation (scrubbing the floors of the dwellings that he once owned) recalls the indignities suffered by Gervaise in Virginie's shop. Closer to Zola's text is Stephen Crane's *Maggie: A Girl of the Streets* (1893), even though the author denied any influence, for not only does Crane's 'Story of New York' follow the model of the plot of *L'Assommoir* but it presents comparable street scenes, describes tenement buildings and incidents of drunken violence, and reproduces the popular speech of the city slums. In Britain also, the example of *L'Assommoir* no doubt provided inspiration for such social novels as Arthur Morrison's *Tales of Mean Streets* (1894) and *A Child of the Jago* (1895) or Gissing's earlier novel on working-class life, *Workers in the Dawn* (1880). Certainly Somerset Maugham's first novel, *Liza of Lambeth* (1897), the story of Liza Kemp, who spurns her Goujet, Tom, and goes off to her undoing with a Lantier figure, the unscrupulous Jim Blakeston, follows closely the pattern of *L'Assommoir*. But the only acknowledged English naturalist novel by the only self-proclaimed naturalist writer in England (at least for one phase in his career) was George Moore's *A Mummer's Wife* (1885), a study of 'temperaments' comparable to *Thérèse Raquin* but also bearing evident traces of the influence of *L'Assommoir*. The heroine of this novel, Kate Ede, who has eloped with the manager of a travelling theatre company, Dick Lennox, is driven to drink. A doctor typically pronounces her an incurable victim of the 'vice of intemperance' and she is left to wander the streets of London, like Gervaise in Paris, until she succumbs to her fate, a 'worn-out machine', 'miserable as a homeless dog', as the narrator describes her, and suffers a characteristic naturalist death. Interestingly, George Moore, in a post-naturalist phase, would return to the pattern of *L'Assommoir* with his best-known novel, *Esther Waters* (1894), in which the seducer of the servant girl, William Latch, the cause of Esther's misfortunes, returns like Lantier to dominate her life. In this novel gambling takes the place of drinking as the source of working-class misery. But, in the end, morality wins the day as Esther's religious faith remains unshakeable and William Latch enjoys a deathbed conversion. The naturalist model provided by Zola's text clearly held such sway that Moore felt obliged to take it up again in order to break with it.

But the importance of a text can be judged not only by critical evaluations and by the extent of its influence on other works, but also by the quantity and variety of reworkings of the same text in adaptations, imitations and parodies. In this regard, Zola's working-class novel was a particularly prolific source. In the immediate aftermath of its publication, then again at the time of the theatrical adaptation by William Busnach and Octave Gastineau, which opened at the Théâtre de l'Ambigu on 18 January 1879 to extraordinary publicity and ran for a whole year, with many successful runs in the provinces and abroad, there was nothing less than a full-scale appropriation of Zola's text by publicists, popular writers and the Parisian public. There were *L'Assommoir* posters, postcards, decorated plates, pantomimes, poems, songs, sketches, parodies. More than a dozen parodies, like *L'Assommoir pour rire*, *Les Gommeux de l'Assommoir*, *L'Assommoir des Marionnettes*, were put on in Paris in 1879 alone. Even Zola, who had secretly collaborated upon the theatrical adaptation, worked for a while on a parody with Busnach, a work which was either lost or never completed. The most notable travesty of the novel, however, was produced beyond the theatre, when, to celebrate the 100th performance of the play, the Ambigu organised a huge costume ball at the Elysée-Montmartre, where all the guests were dressed as working-men or washerwomen and where George Moore dressed as Coupeau was introduced to Zola by Manet. This *L'Assommoir*-mania, which transformed Zola's text into a 'media event', is of more than anecdotal interest. It not only reveals the extraordinary popular success of the work and its impact upon the public, but it also shows how this mimetic text generated its own mimeticism beyond the text. These transpositions of Zola's novel into a lighter vein were both a curious extension of the blithe spirit of the work and, as in the text itself, a denial of the terrible realities that it depicts. It is one of the ironies of the destiny of *L'Assommoir* that it should have been carnivalised in such a way.

Equally revealing were the more serious adaptations of *L'Assommoir*, in which the offensive nature of the original work was masked and the text was appropriated for different ends, usually for the very moralistic purposes that the author had so carefully sought to avoid. From the time of its publication, *L'Assommoir* was subjected to rewritings, reworkings, bowdlerisations, which attest to a more outrageous form of censorship than the outright ban, prompted as they were not by artistic considerations but by ideological motivations directed towards negating the effects of Zola's text. In 1877, for example, the popular novelist Paul Féval wrote *Pierre Blot*, a response to *L'Assommoir*, in which the hero dies of alcoholism but finds his faith on his deathbed. The same year, Achille Secondigné published *Les Kerney-Séverol. Histoire d'une famille française au XIXe siècle. L'Assommé*, a work intended to repair the damage done by *L'Assommoir* by showing workers in a virtuous light. Zola himself was not above making concessions (in private) to public expectations, to secure success in the theatre. In the play, the language is toned down; the plot is adapted to certain melodramatic conventions of the boulevard theatre; Lantier and Virginie take on more the rôle of traitors; and certain characters, even Mes-Bottes, denounce the evils of drink! The Prince of Wales is reported to have thoroughly enjoyed the play on one of his frequent trips to Paris. Indeed it was across the Channel that the most blatant misuses of Zola's text occurred. As Angus Wilson notes, 'the triumph of public morality put a stop to any serious undertaking of the translation of Zola's work into English ... Puritanism and the English law handed it over to the tract vendors' (*Emile Zola*, pp. 149–50). *L'Assommoir* was reduced to the status of such works as a tract by Henry Llewellyn Williams, entitled *Gervaise: A Story of Drink* (1878), in which the heroine is saved from the abyss of alcoholism, marries Goujet and, with their dear little Nana by their side, resolves never to allow Drink to enter their happy home. Charles Reade's dramatisation of *L'Assommoir*, called *Drink* (1879), was, according to Angus Wilson, the 'only serious approach' to the introduction of Zola's works to the British Isles. Yet even Reade's play, which is in fact an adaptation of the French stage adaptation by Busnach and Gastineau (and Zola), is very much in the reformist genre. Gouget (*sic*) declaims against drink outside the 'Assommoir' of Daddy Dove (*sic*) and persuades Coupeau, Mes-Bottes and Bec-Sali (*sic*) to sign the pledge! In this play also, Poisson stabs the traitors, Virginie and Lantier, in a melodramatic dénouement that remains faithful to the recent French drama, but Gervaise is saved, once again thanks to Gou[j]et's intervention. The ardent abstainer has the last word, declaiming, as he clasps Gervaise to his breast: 'Let the wicked tremble and the innocent take heart, for there is a Providence (*lifts hat*) severe, but just.' The original Gervaise would, no doubt, have begged to differ!

The exploitation of Zola's text for temperance propaganda continued on even to the age of the cinema. In France, for example, Ferdinand Zecca produced his (very) short *Les Victimes de l'alcoolisme* (in 1902) before Capellani came out with an adaptation of *L'Assommoir* for the screen (in 1909), one of the very first full-length films to be made, whilst, in the United States, there was *A Drunkard's Reformation, or Saved by a Play*, a temperance melodrama by D. W. Griffith, which, according to Roger Clark (*Zola: 'L'Assommoir'*, p. 81), shows a young man cured of drinking when he sees a stage adaptation of *L'Assommoir*, possibly Reade's *Drink*! Even the most famous film adaptation, René Clément's classic, *Gervaise* (1956), which, to a considerable degree, even in the musical score with its counterpoint of festive and sombre tones, remains faithful to the themes of the text, takes liberties to dilute its effects. In general, for many years after its publication, Zola's novel on drink had to be 'denatured', his *L'Assommoir* 'denaturalised', his powerful potion of a text rendered less potent.

One final repercussion of *L'Assommoir*, and another gauge of its impact on the public, brings us back to the publication of the text, which was a huge commercial success. By the end of November 1877, barely more than ten months after the book had appeared, the 50th edition (of 1,000 copies) was being printed and sales reached 100,000 by the end of 1881. As Henri Mitterand claims, 'Zola thus inaugurated, in the history of the novel, the era of the best-seller' (*Zola. L'histoire et la fiction*, p. 274). According to Maurice Dreyfous, the novelist and his publisher Georges Charpentier had expected the original 4,000 print-run to last for years and were worried that adverse reaction to the novel would damage sales of Zola's other novels. In the event, the phenomenal success of *L'Assommoir* led to a spectacular demand for the novelist's other works. It put his publisher on a firm financial footing; Charpentier gratefully revamped the terms of the novelist's contract. Above all, it made of Zola a best-selling author and a rich man. It is not the least of the ironies of *L'Assommoir* that this 'worthy bourgeois', as Zola described himself in the preface of his novel, should have achieved fame and fortune from his story of the deprivations of his humble heroine and that, from his descriptions of the squalid slums of Paris, he should have acquired the means to buy his country house at Médan and to move to a more comfortable neighbourhood of Paris (rue de Boulogne, now rue Ballu) away from the working-class Batignolles district where he had lived, as his characters might have put it, before 'he made his pile'.

This pivotal novel in Zola's career has nowadays achieved the dual status of a work from another age which continues to have a popular appeal (almost two million copies were sold in the Livre de poche between 1955 and 1981) and yet enjoys the consecration of having become a classic text, a point of reference in histories of French literature, the object of study in academic institutions (even in France) and of much critical attention. It is, however, a text that sits uneasily in the canon, resisting by its remarkable qualities and by its historical significance attempts to exclude it, yet defying by its subject and techniques efforts to incorporate it into traditional schemes. It is a work which also defies attempts to categorise it definitively. Hence, despite its rootedness in a particular setting and a particular age, its openness to new interpretations allows us paradoxically to consider it, if not a modernist text, certainly a work which is admirably suited to the vigour and variety that characterise modern approaches to literature and that prefer, not works that confirm and conform, but texts that constantly provide a new challenge to critic and reader alike.

At one level, *L'Assommoir* remains, very much as Zola himself intended it to be, a realistic description of a slice of contemporary life of which many of his contemporaries preferred not take account. This bold documentary exposé of life in Zola's age has thus acquired considerable historical and ethnographic value in our own, all the more so as the author avoided overt moralising and politicising, thereby ensuring an unusual degree of authenticity for his representation of contemporary life, but revealing nonetheless the profounder ideological presuppositions in which it is grounded. Yet the novel, as an example of Zola's art, is not reducible to any single scheme. In this, as in Zola's works in general, no privileged model prevails, contrary to the claims of the author's theoretical writings. Like other Zola novels also, *L'Assommoir* is forward-looking in its vision of contemporary life, the capitalist, industrial age that it depicts, a world of urban alienation, of massive upheavals with their terrible consequences on anonymous individual lives, of the humiliations of the worker before the tyrannies of the machine, of the unfettered powers of the instinctual unleashed within the shaky constraints of modern civilisation. For F. W. J. Hemmings, Zola was 'the prophet of a new age of mass-psychology, mass-education, and mass-entertainment, an age in which the part is never greater than the whole' (*Emile Zola*, p. 306), an age with its monumental achievements but with its pitiful victims, like Gervaise. With the elements of the classical novel, Zola created a modern anthropology of mythical proportions. But, more so than any other of Zola's texts, *L'Assommoir* is a landmark in its forms and language, not the mere 'treat for linguistic researchers' that Zola presented it as being in his preface, but a veritable logomachy of contending discourses, which, to a considerable degree, breaks down the authority of literary language. Zola no longer merely cites the picturesque jargon of the people like previous writers dealing in their works with the underclasses, but he gives their language an unprecedented centrality in his novel. He thereby reduces the poetic, realistic, descriptive, literary style, to which his readers were accustomed, to a problematic, relative, alien, even ironic status. As Barthes pointedly writes (though not of Zola's work, but of later comparable innovations): 'One can thus see taking shape the possible area of a new humanism: the general suspicion which affects language throughout all modern literature would give way to a reconciliation between the language of the writer and the language of men' (*Le Degré zéro de l'écriture* (Paris: Seuil, 1953), p. 60).

At the same time, *L'Assommoir* remains a compelling novel, because it draws upon the story-teller's intuitive talent for manipulating plot, for creating vivid realistic settings and archetypal situations, with their victims, traitors, martyrs, heroes, grotesque, symbolic figures, the art of involving the reader in the characters' dilemmas; because it derives from the literary craftsman's art of ordering space, forms, techniques, oppositions, repetitions, associations, all to appropriate effect; indeed, because of the whole *tour de force* that it achieves in distilling the most ordinary of subjects into a work of art. Even with its vulgar themes and sordid settings, *L'Assommoir* achieves the appeal of myth, metaphor, symbol, lyricism, a labyrinthine complex of effects brought about by a remarkable circulation of images and by striking interchanges of human, animal and material forms, creative interrelations of the real and the unreal which are the happy result, in this unhappy tale, of the workings of (in Bachelard's term) Zola's 'material imagination'. However grim the atmosphere of the novel, it remains as much a delight for the thematic critic as it is a challenge for the social historian.

Though grounded in the preoccupations of its age, *L'Assommoir* has, nevertheless, retained a lasting actuality. Whatever its political and moral ambiguities, the novel has its own unquestionable morality, the courage, less of its convictions than of its frankness, and, for all the inhumanity of Gervaise's fate, a lasting human, humane appeal. As Edmonde Charles-Roux writes (in *Les Cahiers naturalistes*, 52 (1978), p. 16), 'For as long as there are in this world battered women, young girls thrown out on to the streets, beaten children, exploited workers, we shall always think: *L'Assommoir, Zola.*'

Guide to further reading

Editions and translations of *L'Assommoir*

The standard French edition of *L'Assommoir* appears in Vol. II of the five-volume edition of *Les Rougon-Macquart* in the Bibliothèque de la Pléiade series (Paris: Gallimard, 1961), which is frequently reprinted and contains, as for all the *Rougon-Macquart* novels in this edition, the excellent study and notes by Henri Mitterand (pp. 1532–601). Henri Mitterand has also edited the novel in Vol. III of his edition of Zola's *Œuvres complètes* (Paris: Cercle du livre précieux, 1967), with a preface by R.M. Albérès, and in the Folio series (Paris: Gallimard, 1978), with a preface by Jean-Louis Bory. Incidentally, Zola's preliminary notes for the novel's setting have also been edited by Henri Mitterand in his *Emile Zola. Carnets d'enquêtes* (Paris: Plon, 1986). Among other French editions of the novel itself, the Garnier-Flammarion edition (Paris: 1969), with critical apparatus by Jacques Dubois, is also to be recommended. Of several English translations of *L'Assommoir* that have appeared since 1879, two stand out: the rendering by Arthur Symons, first published in 1895 under the title *L'Assommoir* and frequently reprinted, notably in England by Elek Books of London under the title *The Drunkard*, and the most accessible translation, excellently done by Leonard Tancock, in the Penguin Classics series, under the title *L'Assommoir*, first published in 1970. A complete edition of Zola's correspondence in eleven volumes, eight of which having appeared by 1991, is currently being prepared by a team of Zola scholars under the general editorship of B. H. Bakker and co-published by the Presses de l'Université de Montréal and the Editions du Centre National de la Recherche Scientifique in Paris.

Books and articles specifically on *L'Assommoir*

Three useful introductory studies written in English have recently appeared: *'L'Assommoir': A Working Woman's Life* by Lilian R. Furst (Boston: Twayne, 1990) in 'Twayne's Masterwork Studies' series, focusing heavily on Gervaise's character and fortunes, and *Zola: 'L'Assommoir'* by Roger Clark (University of Glasgow French and German Publications, 1990) in the 'Glasgow Introductory Guides to French Literature' series, no. 13, which is shorter, but more perceptive, with some excellent pages on the novel's setting; finally, *Zola: 'L'Assommoir'* by Valerie Minogue (London: Grant and Cutler, 1991) in the series 'Critical Guides to French Texts'. By far the most important book on the novel is *'L'Assommoir' de Zola. Société, discours, idéologie* by Jacques Dubois (Paris: Larousse, 1973) in the 'Thèmes et textes' series, a remarkable and indispensable study from a variety of critical perspectives, particularly strong on the social and political significance of the text and on Zola's narrative techniques. The other recent books in French are: Jacques Allard's *Zola, le chiffre du texte. Lecture de 'L'Assommoir'* (Montreal, Presses de l'Université de Montréal/Presses universitaires de Grenoble, 1978), a probing structuralist and thematic study, difficult for the uninitiated; in complete contrast, Colette Becker's *'L'Assommoir'. Analyse critique* (Paris: Hatier, 1972), a useful short introductory study intended for students and appearing in the 'Profil d'une œuvre' series (no. 35); finally, *'L'Assommoir'. Emile Zola* (Paris: Nathan, 1989) by Béatrice Desgranges and Patricia Carles in the series 'Balises', a lively introductory study. Two earlier books are now largely of little more than historical interest: *Comment Emile Zola composait ses romans* by Henri Massis (Paris: Fasquelle, 1906), though it does contain a transcription of the preparatory dossier of the novel, housed in the Bibliothèque Nationale in Paris; *La Publication de 'L'Assommoir'* by Léon Deffoux (Paris: Société française d'éditions littéraires et techniques, 1931), which deals with the composition, publication and reception of the work.

Still of considerable interest are certain evaluations of *L'Assommoir* by prominent writers of the past, such as Henri Barbusse in his *Zola* (in French and English; Paris: Gallimard and London: Dent, 1932) and Jean Fréville in his *Zola, semeur d'orages* (Paris: Editions sociales, 1952), or, from the nineteenth century, Francesco De Sanctis in his *Saggi critici*, edited by Luigi Russo (Bari: Laterza, 1952), and J.-K. Huysmans in his articles for *L'Actualité* (Brussels), which appear in English, along with many other theoretical and critical texts dealing with naturalism, in the convenient anthology *Documents of Modern Literary Realism*, edited by George J. Becker (Princeton University Press, 1963).

Several books in English have an informative chapter or section on *L'Assommoir*, among which are such standard works on the French novel as Martin Turnell's *The Art of French Fiction* (London: Hamish Hamilton, 1959) and Harry Levin's more perceptive *The Gates of Horn* (New York and Oxford: Oxford University Press, 1963). Haskell M. Block's *Naturalistic Triptych: The Fictive and the Real in Zola, Mann, and Dreiser* (New York: Random House, 1970) contains useful insights. Gervaise's moral development is intelligently, though not entirely convincingly, analysed in a chapter of *The Moral and the Story* by Ian Gregor and Brian Nicholas (London: Faber and Faber, 1962). Angus Wilson has a chapter on *L'Assommoir* in the collection of his essays entitled *Diversity and Depth in Fiction* and edited by Kerry McSweeney (London: Secker & Warburg, 1983). Phillip A. Duncan studies the paintings in the Louvre episode in *French Literature and the Arts*, edited by Phillip Crant (University of South Carolina Press, 1978) in the *French Literature Series*, Vol. V. Susanna Barrows presents excellent background material on alcoholism and the working classes in *Consciousness and Class Experience in Nineteenth-Century Europe*, edited by John M. Merriman (London and New York: Holmes & Meier, 1979); Roy Jay Nelson is very good on the plot in a chapter of his *Causality and Narrative in French Fiction from Zola to Robbe-Grillet* (Ohio State University Press, 1990). Finally, *L'Assommoir* is the Zola text presented as the 'first working-class novel' and analysed by Sandy Petrey in the *New History of French Literature*, edited by Denis Hollier (Harvard University Press, 1989).

Several journal articles written in English on particular aspects of the novel also deserve to be listed and consulted: Phillip A. Duncan on symbolism (in *The French Review*, October 1980); Edwin Grobe on narrative technique (in *L'Esprit créateur*, Winter 1971); Eunice Lipton on the laundress figure in art and literature (in *Art History*, September 1980); Robert J. Niess on the authenticity of the novel (in *Kentucky Romance Quarterly*, 4 (1979)) and on the use of free indirect speech (in *Nineteenth-Century French Studies*, Fall–Winter 1974–5); David Place on 'the meaning of *L'Assommoir*' (in *French Studies*, January 1974); Sandy Petrey on Goujet as both a God and a worker (in *French Forum*, September 1976); on the same problematic character, Geoff Woollen in articles in the *French Studies Bulletin* (Winter 1981–2) and *Folio* (December 1982); Kathryn Slott on the representation of women in *L'Assommoir* in a special number of *L'Esprit créateur* on 'Zola and Naturalism' (Winter 1985), which also contains an article by Joy Newton and Claude Schumacher in French on the theme of eating; David Baguley on the plot in *PMLA* (October 1975); Robert Lethbridge on the Louvre episode in *The Modern Language Review* (January 1992) and on the songs of the birthday scene in *French Studies* (October 1991). There are other useful thematic studies written in English by Joy Newton on impressionism (with Claude Schumacher) in *L'Esprit créateur* (Winter 1973), on the decline and fall of Gervaise (also with Claude Schumacher) in *Essays in French Literature* (November 1979), and (with Basil Jackson) on point of view technique in *Nineteenth-Century French Studies* (Spring–Summer 1983).

There is a plethora of articles written in French on *L'Assommoir*.

The most selective of listings would necessarily include Henri Mitterand's brilliant study of the genesis of the novel in *Essais de critique génétique* (Paris: Flammarion, 1979), which also appears in a shorter form in his *Le Regard et le signe* (Paris: PUF, 1987), and Philippe Hamon's excellent study of the sites of the novel in *La Goutte d'Or, faubourg de Paris*, edited by Marc Breitman and Maurice Culot (Paris: Hazan, 1988). The open and closed spaces of the novel are studied by Anne Belgrand in *Espaces romanesques*, edited by Michel Crouzet (Paris: PUF, 1982). Annie Goldmann looks at the status of woman in *L'Assommoir* in her *Rêves d'amour perdus* (Paris: Denoël-Gonthier, 1984), Paule Lejeune presents a harsh, left-wing view of the political implications of the novel in her *Histoire et littérature. Les Ecrivains et la politique* (Paris: PUF, 1977). Pierre Boutan surveys the critical reception of the novel in the French press in *Recherches en sciences des textes* (Presses universitaires de Grenoble, 1977). Henri Guillemin has an informative chapter on *L'Assommoir* in his *Présentation des 'Rougon-Macquart'* (Paris: Gallimard, 1964). Janice Best studies the French stage version of the novel in her book *Expérimentation et adaptation* (Paris: José Corti, 1986).

Les Cahiers naturalistes, the specialised journal of studies on Zola and naturalism, have published several studies on *L'Assommoir*, notably in no. 52 (1978), which includes nine articles on the novel from the proceedings of an important conference and from the annual 'pilgrimage' to Médan of 1977 on the occasion of the centennial commemorations. Other useful articles in the same journal include studies on the moral of *L'Assommoir* (by Jeanne Gaillard in no. 54 (1980)), on *L'Assommoir*, Eugène Manuel, Arthur Ranc, and *Le Sublime* (by Geoff Woollen in no. 56 (1982)), on the novel's style (by Jean-Louis Vissière in no. 11 (1958)), its vocabulary (by Simone Bonnafous in no. 55 (1981)), and its repetitions (by R. Butler in no. 57 (1983)), as well as studies on the themes of water (by Marie-José Cassard and Pascale Joinville in no. 55 (1981)) and 'destructuration' (by Patricia Carles in no. 63 (1989)). Other journal articles in French that deserve special mention are the studies of the language of the novel by Marcel Cressot (in *Le Français moderne*, June–July 1940) and Martine Léonard (in *Etudes françaises*, February 1974), the thorough consideration of the influence of Poulot's *Le Sublime* by Pierre Cogny (in the *Cahiers de l'Association internationale des études françaises*, May 1972) and Richard L. Barnett's article on the poetics of disintegration in the novel (in *Romance Notes*, Winter 1987).

General studies on Zola and Naturalism

The best general study of Zola and his works in English remains the second, revised edition of *Emile Zola* by F. W. J. Hemmings (Oxford: Clarendon Press, 1966). Graham King's *Garden of Zola: Emile Zola and his Novels for English Readers* (London: Barrie & Jenkins/New York, Barnes & Noble, 1978), despite its limitations, is an informative, readable book for the general public. Of a number of recent biographies in English, Philip Walker's *Zola* (London: Routledge & Kegan Paul, 1985) is the best. Angus Wilson's *Emile Zola: An Introductory Study of his Novels* (London: Secker & Warburg, 1952) is a lively general study written from a broadly Freudian standpoint, which has frequently been reissued. Naomi Schor's *Zola's Crowds* (Johns Hopkins University Press, 1978) is a stimulating modern reading of Zola's works. The recent collective volume *Zola and the Craft of Fiction (Essays in Honour of F. W. J. Hemmings)* (Leicester University Press, 1990), edited by Robert Lethbridge and Terry Keefe, contains a variety of interesting studies from different critical perspectives in both English and French, with numerous references to and a whole chapter (by Joy Newton) on *L'Assommoir*. *Naturalism* by Lilian R. Furst and Peter N. Skrine (London: Methuen, 1971) is a brief introduction to the field of naturalist literature in 'The Critical Idiom' series, no. 18. For a more detailed study that focuses on naturalist fiction as a distinct literary genre, see David Baguley's more recent *Naturalist Fiction: The Entropic Vision* (Cambridge University Press, 1990).

Of the many books on Zola and his works written in French, Guy Robert's classic *Emile Zola: principes et caractères généraux de son œuvre* (Paris: Les Belles Lettres, 1952) is still well worth consulting, and Marc Bernard's standard introduction *Zola par lui-même*, first published the same year, has recently been updated by Jean-Pierre Leduc-Adine as *Zola* (Paris: Seuil, 1988). Two relevant introductory studies have also recently been published in the handy 'Que sais-je?' series (Paris: PUF): *Zola et le naturalisme* (1986) by Henri Mitterand and *Le Naturalisme* (1989) by Alain Pagès. Yves Chevrel's *Le Naturalisme* (Paris: PUF, 1982) is an important innovative general study of naturalist literature. More specialised approaches are to be found in Jean Borie's psychoanalytical study, *Zola et les mythes, ou de la nausée au salut* (Paris: Seuil, 1971), in Neide de Faria's structuralist, narratological analysis of a corpus of Zola novels (including *L'Assommoir*), *Structures et unité dans 'Les Rougon-Macquart'* (Paris: Nizet, 1977), in Auguste Dezalay's study of rhythm and repetition, *L'Opéra des 'Rougon-Macquart'* (Paris: Klincksieck, 1983), in Roger Ripoll's wide-ranging and thorough-going work on *Réalité et mythe chez Zola* (Paris: Champion, 1981), and in the brilliant study of the (thermo) dynamics of Zola's *Rougon-Macquart* series by Michel Serres, *Feux et signaux de brume. Zola* (Paris: Grasset, 1975). Maurice Dreyfous, in *Ce qu'il me reste à dire* (Paris: Ollendorff, 1913), presents interesting anecdotes on Zola's career as a writer, and in Henri Mitterand's *Zola. L'Histoire et la fiction* (Paris: PUF, 1990) there is a useful history of the French editions of Zola's works.

Bibliographies

For further study and research on Zola and his works, the following bibliographies are recommended: Brian Nelson, *Emile Zola: A Selective Analytical Bibliography* (London: Grant & Cutler, 1982), a compact reference work with short, annotated entries on criticism up to the end of 1979; the chapter on Zola by Philip Walker and David Baguley, containing over 400 annotated entries on criticism up to the end of 1989, in the forthcoming *Critical Bibliography of French Literature: The Nineteenth Century* (Syracuse University Press), edited by David Baguley; the two volumes of the *Bibliographie de la critique sur Emile Zola* (Toronto University Press, 1976 and 1982) by David Baguley, covering the periods 1864–1970 and 1971–80, with more than 9,000 (unannotated) entries; supplements to these bibliographies appear annually in *Les Cahiers naturalistes*.